EXTENSION OF RICOEUR'S HERMENEUTIC

Dedicated to
My Mary

EXTENSION OF RICOEUR'S HERMENEUTIC

by

PATRICK L. BOURGEOIS

MARTINUS NIJHOFF / THE HAGUE / 1975

PRINTED IN THE NETHERLANDS

TABLE OF CONTENTS

ACKNOWLEDGEMENTS

I am deeply grateful to Eugene O. Bourgeois Sr., my father, for his expert help with the French and German languages and the texts used in this manuscript. However, all responsibility for any inaccuracies in translation are my responsibility.

I am indebted to Loyola University of New Orleans for a grant given by the Academic Grants Committee to defray expenses of preparing the final manuscript.

I express my gratitude to Mrs. Eugenie Klopf Cronan for the tedious task of typing the final manuscript.

I would like to express my appreciation to the editor and director of *Research in Phenomenology* for allowing me to republish the following article: "Phenomenology and the Sciences of Language," vol. I, pp. 119-136.

I would also like to express my appreciation to the editor of *Philosophy Today* for allowing me to republish the following article: "Hermeneutics of Symbols and Philosophical Reflection: Paul Ricœur," Winter 1971, pp. 231-241.

October 10, 1974

P. L. B.

INTRODUCTION

The path Husserl entered upon at the beginning of his philosophical writings turned out to be the beginning of a long, tedious way. Throughout his life he constantly comes to grips with the fundamental problems which set him upon this path. Beginning with the logical level of meaning, laboring through the idealism of the transcendental phenomenology of the period between *Ideas I* to the *Meditations*, in search for the ever more originary, he finally arrived at the level of the *Lebenswelt*. It was this later focus on the ever more originary, the source, the foundation of meaning which led him finally to the horizon of meaning and the genesis of meaning in the *Lebenswelt* period. This later period allows for a quasi wedding of his phenomenology with some adaptation of existentialism. But this union called for an adaptation of Husserl's logistic prejudice.

The period of the *Lebenswelt* allows many of the later phenomenologists to speak of the failure of the brackets in their extreme exclusion and to allow for a link between man and his world in the *Lebenswelt*. This link is at the source of the ontological investigations and theories which arise from the phenomenological movement. However, there is the possibility of many tensions in such an endeavor since the study of being can be most abstract and most concrete. This treatise purports to investigate one of those manners of access to ontology, that of the French philosopher, Paul Ricœur. Ricœur considers the access to ontology a difficult one. Man's link to being is not easily gained without loosing many important aspects of that bond.

Husserl had begun his long, steady trek at the logical level and throughout his life worked toward the more originary, the source, the *Ursprung*. In the period of the *Lebenswelt*, it can be made clear that this origin is not immediately accessible and must therefore be reached indirectly by questioning back, what has become known as the *Rückfrage*. Ricœur still holds fast to this necessity of a *Rückfrage* to arrive at the originary, at the

Ursprung. Therefore, when he takes up the problem of the will, he considers it necessary to begin with the eidetic level and work back to the *Ursprung*, to continuously get closer and closer to the origin in its concrete fullness. His direction is therefore from the eidetic to the empirical, which, even from the beginning of his philosophy of the will, he considered accessible from a treatment of a mythics. But Ricœur is hesitant to move too quickly through this mythical level to an explicitly ontological level. He constantly takes detours before arriving at this final stage. The first general obvious detour which he considers necessary is the detour through the symbolics, the detour through the hermeneutics of symbols.

This treatise will attempt to take up some of the problems emerging from the development of Ricœur's philosophy. He has begun his philosophy of the will with a treatment of the structures of willing using an eidetic method of description. When he works out some of the problems of interpretation, reflection, and hermeneutics, he learns that all reflection is interpretation. Thus the question emerges as to whether the first level of treatment of the philosophy of the will is also to some extent hermeneutical.

In order to render a treatment of this question, it is necessary first to present the manner of Ricœur's initial undertaking on this eidetic level of the will. Then an account of his development to his new position must be rendered. Does he really change his initial position or is it simply a matter of something which he only grasped implicitly becoming more explicit? In other words, can we say that his first treatment on the level of pure reflection is implicitly hermeneutical? And if it is not, should it be?

Chapter one of this treatment will present a lengthy statement of these problems. Chapter two will attempt to explicate the eidetic phase of Ricœur's method, the eidetic treatment of the structures of the will. Chapter three will thoroughly investigate his too often neglected pure reflection on the existential structures of disproportion of fallible man making possible the fault and underlying the empirics of man. And Chapter four attempts to make the transition from the level of pure reflection to Ricœur's confrontation with hermeneutics. Chapter five will treat his basic theory of symbols and hermeneutics, and the conflict of interpretation within the field of interpretation. Chapters six and seven will attempt to deal with some of the detours, deepenings, and extensions he has had to make. This treatment of these encounters will make it clear to some extent how Ricœur has had to extend his initial views, and lead to a concluding chapter. This concluding chapter will attempt to confront further these problems of extensions and return to the first stages of his philosophy of will, and thus answer the questions posed in the first chapter. Since the first chapter presents a lengthy statement of these problems with the aim of this study, it is not necessary to deal with them any further in this introduction.

CHAPTER I

STATEMENT OF THE PROBLEM

RECENT EXPANSION

Few thinkers take their initial ideas or insights through different stages of development without some deepening, change or extension. The unfolding of the initial insight is not clearly foreseen at the beginning. This is especially true for philosophical thinking which wants to work back toward its starting point. The tendency is to continually renew the initial insight in the light of further development. This tendency to renewal in the starting point can easily lead superficial readers to stand detached and at a distance from the thinker's development and accuse him of a radical change in relation to his insight and starting point. A victim on the contemporary philosophical scene of this accusation of radical change is Martin Heidegger. Some would see a radical change in his philosophy from the early stage of *Sein und Zeit* [1] to his later writings, instead of seeing how he entered upon his path, continued to make headway along that path, and focused more explicitly on his initial question of the meaning of Being.

The concern of this study is of such a philosopher, Paul Ricœur. In the first stage of his *Philosophy of the Will* he could see in general his project in its entirety, as is clear from the introduction of *Le volontaire et l'involontaire*.[2] However, once he began the long trek down that path, the specific direction to be travelled and problems to be met became clearer. Consequently he encountered some problems which he did not fully and explicitly grasp at the outset. Questions therefore at the later stage of his philosophy of the will might well be asked concerning the changes which the later stages necessitate in the first stage. Some of the themes and extensions which have explicitly emerged can be seen implicitly in the initial stages. And in the new light of their having become explicit, one might

[1] Martin Heidegger, *Sein und Zeit* (Max Niemeyer Verlag: Tübingen, 1963).
[2] Paul Ricœur, *Philosophie de la volonté*, Vol. I. *Le volontaire et l'involontaire*. English ed., trans. by Erazim V. Kohak. References to this work will be in VI.

consider the possibility of a need for a radical revision of the initial stage
of his philosophy of the will.

One such implicit orientation in Ricœur's first stage, the eidetic stage of
his philosophy of the will, is the turn to a hermeneutic phenomenological
method in order to reach a concrete reflection. Ricœur in the introduction
to *Le volontaire et l'involontaire* (VI, 27) does even at the outset see the
need to turn to such an hermeneutical method. In fact, even then he
considered the eidetic stage as the necessary prolegomenon to the empirics
and the poetics.[3] (VI, 36) Only later does the conflict within the hermeneutical field emerge and become problematic. The questions to which
this hermeneutical stage gives rise concerning the initial stages of his philosophy of the will cannot be avoided.

The first question of this treatise flows from this last and more recent
stage of Ricœur's work, the hermeneutic stage. His philosophy of the will
has reached the level of concrete reflection. At this stage reflection becomes interpretation. However, at this stage it also becomes clear to him
that all reflection is interpretation. The further question therefore emerges:
is this a radical about-face? Does this view mean a complete change from
the first phase which is eidetic and therefore a pure reflection which tries to
arrive at the structures of willing? To what extent does Ricœur in coming to
grips with the hermeneutical problems with its conflicts, in resolving the
conflict the way in which he does it, find it necessary to alter his initial
study? Or is it the case that in making explicit some of the initial orientations, a return can be made to the eidetic stage in such a way as to
understand and shake loose certain impulses and hidden aspects which are
only accessible now after the further development and deepening to concrete reflection? In other words, to what extent does the development call
for a change in the return to the initial stage? It is clear that Ricœur has
changed in his view of the nature of philosophy as reflection, and has found
it necessary to extend his views of symbols, of language and of interpretation.

Thus this treatise is a *Rückfrage* in the sense of a questioning back from
the later hermeneutical stage of his philosophy of the will to the initial
stage. The questioning back is intended to bring to light and make explicit
Ricœur's development as consistent and as continuous in spite of some

---

[3] In the use of such substantives as empirics, eidetics, symbolics, mythics, poetics,
we are attempting to render Ricœur's use of the same words as substantives: *l'em-
pirique, l'eidétique, la symbolique, le mythique, la poétique.* In such usage we are
following Charles Kelbley in his translation of Ricœur's *Philosophie de la volonté,*
Vol. II. *Finitude et culpabilité,* Part I: *L'homme faillible.* This work shall be referred
to as HF. See his footnote concerning this usage in *Fallible Man,* p. X.

radical expansions. It also aims at making certain initial implicit themes more explicit.

It is clear that Ricœur at the outset of his project on the will did not consider the eidetic stage of the philosophy of the will to be interpretation. He considered it to be immediate reflection.[4] It was an eidetics of the will as the bracketing of the fact and elaborating of the essence (VI, 7) and an intentional analysis in order to arrive at the structures of willing.

However, if we look back from the hermeneutical stages, returning in a *Rückfrage* to the initial stage, will it not emerge as implicitly hermeneutical? Is this the way Ricœur considers it? This is the theme we shall attempt to develop and illuminate; that there has been at least an implicit hermeneutics in the eidetics of the will; that structural understanding is also interpretation. In order to render an account of the continuity and constancy in Ricœur's thinking, it will be necessary to bring to light certain developments, deepenings and even changes in the initial impulses of his passage to concrete reflection from eidetic or pure reflection. Thus we are involved in a circle. To show continuity, it is necessary to bring discontinuity, change and expansion to light. In order to show the fundamental continuity and extent of Ricœur's hermeneutical phenomenology, it is necessary to consider the change he undergoes with regard to the question of the origin of meaning.

Now that Ricœur looks back after the long detour to work out the problem of the conflict of interpretation, and after developing more explicitly his theory of signs, this question of the extent of its hermeneutical method can more easily be posed to his first eidetic stage. The whole consideration springs from a change in view to which his first hermeneutical endeavor gave rise. He came to realize in his *La symbolique du mal* [5] that man is not the only responsible agent of evil but that he is also victim. In *La symbolique du mal* he defends a position which reflects a changed view. In the first stage, he emphasized the role of the voluntary as source of meaning. Therefore man would be the totally responsible origin of evil. This emphasis is clear from the introduction of *Le volontaire et l'involontaire* (p. 8-9). The relation of the voluntary and the involuntary is intelligible. Description is understood by means of their relation.

The reciprocity of the voluntary and the involuntary does not even leave

---

[4] Paul Ricœur, *De l'interprétation, Essai sur Freud*, p. 443. The reference to this work will be DI. Ricœur repeats constantly throughout VI that the eidetics attempts to be pure reflection. This shall be treated at greater length at the beginning of Chapter two.

[5] Paul Ricœur, *Philosophie de la volonté.* Vol. II. *Finitude et culpabilité*, Part II: *La symbolique du mal.* Hereafter referred to as SM.

any doubt about the sense in which it is necessary to read their relation. Not only does the involuntary not have any meaning of its own, but the understanding proceeds from the top to below and not from below to the above. Far from being able to derive the voluntary from the involuntary, it is on the contrary the understanding of the voluntary which is first in man. (VI, 8-9).

It is this altered emphasis which we hope will bring to light in a more fundamental manner the source of all the detours for Ricœur. It is not merely after *La symbolique du mal* that Ricœur turned to Freud and his manner of interpreting symbols and to semiology and linguistics. Rather, it is precisely because of the endeavor of *La symbolique du mal*, its method, and its insights on evil and the receptivity of the will to evil already there, which brings him to see fuller and deeper implications of the primitive receptivity of the voluntary from the involuntary as also a reception of meaning, and not just a giving of meaning to motive and organs and situations.[6]

Nevertheless, Ricœur does not wish to give up his theory of the abstraction of fault and innocence. He still considers it possible and necessary to come to the basic structures of human will as he did in *Le volontaire et l'involontaire* and *L'homme faillible*. But how can he keep from having to forfeit his descriptive stage of structures? How does he, after developing the fuller theory of signs, attempt to preserve his structural phenomenology as abstract description of structures of willing? Now that the involuntary must be considered more important because it has its own meaning and is the source of meaning in desire and spirit, is it possible to preserve a pure description? In what manner, if any, is the eidetic possible and necessary as a preliminary treatment of willing, since now he sees more clearly the indirect access to these structures?

A further difficulty presents itself. In *Le volontaire et l'involontaire* Ricœur made great efforts to present an abstract man with a constant, invariable nature. The problem emerges, in the light of his view of the deepened origin of meaning and the role of the involuntary, as to whether or not this constant nature can still be maintained. Does the decentering of consciousness as the total source of meaning, the altered view of the phenomenological reduction, necessitate a change in this view of man?

---

[6] Paul Ricœur, *Le conflit des interprétations, Essais d'herméneutique,* p. 260, this will be referred to as CI.

CORRELATED PROBLEMS

Throughout the development of this study which shall be an attempt to question back to discover the extent of hermeneutics in Ricœur's phenomenology of the will, certain other problems will arise. These are problems which Ricœur has had to deal with throughout his own development. This treatment must come to grips with the question of precisely why, in the light of his fundamental concerns, Ricœur has had to turn to the objective sciences of man and of signs in general. It is in seeing his need to turn to these sciences that it will finally become more clear to what extent his philosophy is hermeneutical, and also to what extent he can and does still preserve the eidetic stage of the philosophy of the will as not only possible but also necessary.

However, in hindsight, he can see more clearly the nature of his prior undertaking. Although it will perhaps be necessary to see that undertaking in a new light as implicit hermeneutics, in that way it is brought to light in the context of his own explication of certain of its themes. It will be discovered that this "destruction" and reconstruction is the result of his fundamental working hypothesis: to turn to concrete reflection in the empirics of the will and the problems it entails. (CI, 260)

STATUS OF REPRESENTATION

The role of representation in Ricœur's philosophy of the will places us at the center of his philosophy. This role must be unfolded in its connection or bond to effort and desire, in its relation to deeds or acts and signs and phantasms: i.e., in a word, to the relation between the "will and its signs." [7] The question is thus posed as Ricœur himself wishes to pose it: ". . . . It is now the status of the representation in the reflective method which raises the question." (CI, 212)

According to Ricœur, Husserl considered affective and volitive processes of the human subject to be processes founded on representation. This makes representation primary and founding and these processes founded. Ricœur considers the role of representation to be just the reverse. (CI, 211) Representation is not the first function but the second. The first and primary is desire and effort, willing, and the representation is founded. This reversal makes these functions founding and the representation takes on the character as founded. And Ricœur's interpretation then takes on

[7] Paul Ricœur, "Terry Lectures" Third lecture, p. 10. Yale University in 1961. These lectures appear substantially in DI and in CI.

the tone of a movement from founded representation to founding desire and spirit. For Ricœur it is this view which makes Husserl guilty of the primacy of theoretical knowledge or of what Ricœur calls his "logicism" [8] or logistic prejudice.

He did not see as clearly as he does today the differences with Husserl on this point of the founded character of the representation. The development and deepening of this founded character of the representation, after his confrontation with Nabert and Freud, and his admission of influences on meaning from sources other than immediate consciousness, will take up our attention as this treatment unfolds.

Some fundamental polarities and tensions will come to light by keeping in mind the fundamental relation between representation and signs. For it is precisely here at the juncture of signs and will that reflection means interpretation: i.e., interpreting signs (of willing) becomes reflection and vice versa. This bond between signs and will also sheds some light on Ricœur's conviction of the necessity to turn critically to those sciences which try to decipher and to interpret the signs of man ". . . to include the results, the methods and the presuppositions . . ." of these sciences.[9]

Three further points should be considered in this focusing on the role of representation. First, the basic question of this work cannot be lost sight of. It is by considering the various connections of representation, its relation to the conflict of interpretation, its role in Ricœur's philosophy of language, its place in acts and signs, that the theme will gradually be unfolded to answer the questions of this treatise: to what extent is Ricœur's philosophy of the will hermeneutical, in the light of his changed emphasis, and in hindsight? What does his recent extension and change mean for the stage of pure description and eidetic? The question is whether or not he still needs the eidetic or whether he wishes to do away with that stage altogether, as irreconcilable to his position favoring hermeneutic as opposed to a structural approval, with its emphasis on tradition, change and history. All these reverberations will hopefully reach a climatic resolution in the perspective of Ricœur's final arrival at his goal, after traveling the path of his long way, the general hermeneutic of the "I am."

The second point to be considered in focusing on the role of representation is the adequacy or actual centrality of this focus. The role of representation will be at the center of consideration of several of the following chapters. This role will be considered in its most general relation: the

---

[8] Paul Ricœur, *Husserl, an Analysis of his Phenomenology*, ed. and trans. by Edward G. Ballard and Lester E. Embree, pp. 5, 8, 16, and 17, *passim*.

[9] Paul Ricœur, Third "Terry Lecture," p. 11.

bond of man to being, the bond of the word or symbol to being, the paradoxes and conflicts to which this bond expressed in language of symbols gives rise, and finally its role in the concrete symbol as basis of the concrete reflection which Ricœur considers to be the working hypothesis of his whole philosophy. (CI, 260). Then its role will come to light in our conclusion as also related to the reflection on structure, a reflection which is implicitly hermeneutical.

It is necessary to mention at this point, however, that although this role of representation is a central focus it will not necessarily be the explicit focus of each chapter. Its centrality will not fully emerge until the end of this treatment.

The third point: It will be necessary to relate the role of representation to another theme throughout the development of this work. It would be a precarious procedure to attempt by means of the role of representation to enter the philosophy of Ricœur at its center, and to fail to consider the fundamental theme or thematic of his whole undertaking, the problem of evil and reconciliation. This is the problem which prompted his philosophy of the will even at its first stage. And it is not merely by chance that the fourth part of his recent publication, *Le conflit des interprétations,* has as its title "La symbolique du mal interprété." Nor is it by chance that the last part of the same work is in the realm of the hermeneutic and *poetics* of religious symbols. In the context of our problematic, the question arises and will hopefully be answered during the development of this treatise, as to why Ricœur has returned to *La symbolique du mal* only after such a long delay. Or, more precisely, why did he have to detour and delay for so long from the conclusion of that work, "Le symbole donne à penser," and the return to that theme to carry it forward to the level of "penser"? This problem will be constantly in the background in the consideration of primitive receptivity in the relation of the voluntary and the involuntary, in the possibility of the fault in disproportion, in the servile will, and in the origin and source of meaning as emphasizing the involuntary on the level of concrete reflection.

PROCEDURE OF TREATMENT

The first step will be a treatment of Ricœur's eidetic phenomenology and pure reflection and their limits. After this an attempt shall be made to place the role of representation in Ricœur's phenomenology of language and his phenomenology of signs. The limits of his philosophy of language, the path he takes to originary language and to poetics, will bring to light the cause of many problems he encounters on the "long way" he takes. (CI, 14). It is within his phenomenology of symbolic language that the problems of hermeneutics, the conflict of hermeneutics, the solution to the conflict in concrete hermeneutics and concrete reflection come to light in their original roots. In the process of such considerations we must turn to language as the sciences of language view it. Then we shall return to thematise our initial question of the meaning of his various extensions and their relevance to the first stages of his philosophy of the will.

Throughout this work we shall be proceeding under the guidance of Ricœur's own development. First we shall turn to his structural phenomenology and see what Ricœur wanted to do and how he argued for such an eidetic description of structures of willing, yielding an abstract man. Such a consideration of the level of eidetic and pure reflection will take us to his *Le volontaire et l'involontaire* and *L'homme faillible*. The limits of these levels of pure description must be brought to the fore especially in relation to the problem of evil. This consideration of pure reflection in his philosophy of the will takes up the next three chapters.

After such a consideration of the level of pure reflection, we will consider Ricœur's turn to the empirics of the will in the hermeneutic of symbols. In order to work out this hermeneutical level we shall begin with a lengthy treatment of the theory of symbols and hermeneutics presupposed by the empirics of the will as it unfolds in *La symbolique du mal*. This theory of symbols and interpretation will lead us into the realm of the conflict of interpretations which it has become necessary for Ricœur to encounter. It also brings up his confrontation with the linguists and other sciences of language in an attempt to articulate these sciences together with a phenomenological language and hermeneutics. Thus we see that this treatment must bring to the fore Ricœur's confrontation with the challenge presented by what he calls semiology, including in this science of signs both psychoanalysis and linguistic sciences. This treatment hopefully will bring to light his further development of a theory of signs, symbols, and interpretation which is the basis of re-interpreting the first levels of reflection as implicitly hermeneutics.

Finally, after following this path, we hope to make a return to the eidetics treated at the beginning and render the problems posed in this chapter in terms of some solution. From the development it should become clear to what extent Ricœur has remained constant to his initial impulse in his philosophy of will, to what extent he has had to change, and to what extent he can maintain the descriptions of *Le volontaire et l'involontaire,* and especially to what extent and in what sense his phenomenology of the will is already hermeneutical. Furthermore, the problems of his poetics shall become more clear, i.e., the problem he has had in search of a language of metaphor. After he has incarnated the poetics in the oneiric, (DI, 503), creativity in receiving from desire, how can he engage in creative interpretation of symbols?

SUMMARY

In summary, then, the questions of this treatise are: (1) What are the implications of Ricœur's recent "extension" of interpretation, of symbol, of text for his pure reflective stage of his philosophy of the will, or to what extent is Ricœur's philosophy of the will hermeneutical; (2) to what extent has he changed his position from *Le volontaire et l'involontaire* or eidetic level or reflection; (3) to what extent does this changed attitude affect his initial stage and preserve it; (4) what in his phenomenology makes it possible for him, and necessary at the same time, to turn to the objective sciences to include critically their results; (5) how does all this relate to the fundamental thematic of his philosophy of will, the problem of evil, and the promise of reconciliation and salvation?

CHAPTER II

EIDETICS AND ITS LIMITS

INTRODUCTION

Our first focus in working out the question of the extent of the hermeneutical character of reflection in the philosophy of Ricœur is on his structural or eidetic phenomenology. We shall in this first focus attempt to present this level as he initially engaged in it. Only after treating his later turn to the concrete hermeneutical reflection can we return and reveal its implicit hermeneutical character, as well as its necessarily explicit hermeneutical character. But in order to pose the problem properly in its undistorted tension and to polarize the different perspectives on this eidetic level, we will attempt to treat this level from the perspective of pure reflection undistorted by the turn and passage to hermeneutics and concrete reflection.

LIMITS OF EIDETICS

This chapter will attempt to specify the limits of an eidetic phenomenology of the will. It considers the first level as Ricœur did when he engaged in it. Therefore, the advantages and need for a treatment of the structures as common to the fallen and to the innocent man are considered. In this way, it is hoped, the ground will be laid for later dealing with the question of continuity and change more clearly. For, if Ricœur has found it necessary to alter his position, the question of the necessity or the possibility of this treatment of structures arises.

PHENOMENOLOGY OF THE WILL WITHIN EIDETIC LIMITS

The mainstream of Paul Ricœur's philosophical development has unfolded in reanimating certain questions of the problem of the will in a return to the philosophical origins of this problem. He sees this problem revitalized in the form of three questions.[1] The first is the question of human act, or the conditions of existence of a responsible subject; the second is the relation between this human act and the whole of nature, or in Kantian terms, the question of the causality of nature and the causality of freedom, which Ricœur calls the question of motivation; the third is the question of the ultimate nature of human freedom as human freedom. This threefold reanimation of the questions of human act, motivation, and human freedom is what Ricœur has taken up in his philosophy of the will.

Ricœur's phenomenology of the will must be considered in the light of his attitude toward Husserl's phenomenology and its different stages of development.[2] He is at this stage especially convinced of the importance of Husserl's phenomenology in its totality and not just that within the period of the *Lebenswelt*. He wants to emphasize the importance of Husserl's logical works, his works of intuition, those of the transcendental reduction, as well as those of the period of the *Lebenswelt*. In fact, he harshly criticizes those existential phenomenologists who have gone too quickly to the last period of Husserl without doing justice to the first stage. Thus it should be clear that in his early stage of developing phenomenology of the will he considers himself closer than the existential phenomenologists to the earlier stage of Husserl.

Several points of contact emerge between these two phenomenological undertakings reflecting what Ricœur considers to be his legacy from Husserl. The first emerges by way of difference or contrast. Ricœur is constantly referring to what he calls Husserl's logicism or logistic prejudice. However, on the positive side, phenomenology of the will owes to Husserl its descriptive analysis, eidetics, and intentionality; i.e., "Intentionality on the one hand, and reference to a self on the other." (VI, 12). Also, imaginative variation, and essence or *eidos* play a large part in Ricœur's phenomenology of the will. The first to be taken up here is Husserl's limitation of phenomenology or his logical prejudice.

Husserl's Logicism

Husserl's logical prejudice would emphasize the theoretical consciousness at the expense of the practical and the affective consciousness, founding these latter on the former. Ricœur violently disagrees with founding the practical and the affective on the theoretical acts, and presents an intentional analysis beginning with the noema or noematic correlate of these

[1] Paul Ricœur, "Philosophy of Will and Action," in *Phenomenology of Will and Action,* ed. by Erwin W. Straus and Richard M. Griffith, p. 8.

[2] Paul Ricœur, "New Developments in Phenomenology in France: The Phenomenology of Language," *Social Research,* Vol. 34, 1967, p. 2.

acts. This shall be elaborated further in the next chapters in the context of the founded character of representation and the priority of the "I can" over the "I see."

The first level of Ricœur's phenomenology of the will takes place as an eidetics of the will. He speaks of the abstraction of this level as close to Husserl's eidetic reduction, as "Putting in parentheses of the fact and elaborating the idea or sense." (VI, 7). For Ricœur, such a reduction, or a reduction of some kind, is the means of entrance to phenomenology.[3] For him, phenomenology means the science of appearances or of appearings, which becomes strict when the status of the appearing of things becomes problematical.[4] It becomes strict when asked the question, "What does 'appearing' signify for a thing, for an animate being, for a person, for a conscious experience, for a feeling? . . ." [5] Thus it is clear that the reduction is of considerable importance for Ricœur's philosophy of the will at its first level, which he considers to be an eidetic reflection.

For Husserl the eidetic and its reduction held a place of special importance. First, the phenomenological *epoché* has "put out of action" or "placed in brackets" all transcendence of intentionality of consciousness, of all the fact-world.[6] The phenomenological *epoché* has delivered us from the natural attitude to what is immanent in consciousness; this he calls the phenomenological residue. In the words of Ricœur's commentary on this point, "the reduction would be a reduction of transcendence, that is, of everything which, being other than consciousness, is there for it." [7]

A clearer statement of his eidetic reduction and phenomenology is found in Husserl's *Encyclopaedia Britannica* article,[8] which states the importance of reductions. "The proper starting-point for the systematic unravelling of this science lies in the chapter (of *Ideas*) which treats of the reductions. . . ." [9] However, in this discussion, one must remember that eidetics, which is of primary interest in this context, is for Husserl only one stage toward his transcendental ego, a stage toward which he has already arrived

---

[3] Paul Ricœur, "Kant and Husserl" in *An Analysis of his Phenomenology*, trans. by Edward G. Ballard and Lester E. Embree, p. 176.

[4] Paul Ricœur, "Existential Phenomenology" in *Husserl: An Analysis of his Phenomenology*, p. 207.

[5] *Ibid.*, p. 202.

[6] Edmund Husserl, *Ideen*, p. 56.

[7] Paul Ricœur, *Edmund Husserl, Idées directrices pour une phénoménologie*, p. 102.

[8] Edmund Husserl, "Phenomenology," *Encyclopaedia Britannica*, Ed. 14, Vol. 17, pp. 699-702.

[9] Edmund Husserl, *Ideas, General Introduction to Pure Phenomenology*, p. 6.

in a preliminary way by the period of his *Ideas*, but at which he only fully arrives later.

For a fuller elaboration of the reduction and eidetics of Husserl, it is necessary to grasp in some preliminary fashion his doctrine of intentionality. For Husserl, "all consciousness is intentional." [10] "It is intentionality which characterizes consciousness in the pregnant sense of the term and justifies us in describing the whole stream of experience as at once a stream of consciousness and unity of one consciousness." [11] Thus for Husserl, consciousness is clearly and fundamentally characterized by its function of referring, of tendency toward an object, as a consciousness of ... and an intentional experience cannot for Husserl be described without describing what in the experience is the object of consciousness. Thus, with the *epoché*, not the world, but the "sense" of the world appears. In the phenomenological bracketing, in which the natural attitude is relinquished, the description is of what then appears, the *noema* in the *noesis*.[12]

The phenomenological reduction has yielded the phenomena of actual internal experience. The eidetic reduction brings us one stage further toward the transcendental ego, revealing the essential forms constraining psychical existence. The eidetic level is the level of the essential structure, the invariable structures of consciousness. When Ricœur speaks of the first stage of his phenomenology of the will as eidetic, he refers to it in the sense of looking for the essential structures of willing, deciding, etc.

The *eidos* for Ricœur just as for Husserl can be obtained in their purity through free fancy or imaginative variation, to which Ricœur refers constantly and upholds as a still viable aspect of Husserl's phenomenology. From some particular experiences he wishes to come to those constants of the particulars, to their essential structures. Thus imaginative variation plays a primary part in Ricœur's eidetics of the will. At the time of *Le volontaire et l'involontaire*, he holds with Husserl to the intuition of these essential structures, to their immediate grasp and understanding by description.[13] Thus he is not after the daily forms of human willing, since these present themselves as ramifications and distortions of certain fundamental structures which are the essential structures. (VI, 7). These for Ricœur as well as for Husserl are the a priori structures of all lived experiences.

Thus Ricœur, to get away from the distortion of the everyday form of

---

[10] Edmund Husserl, *Encyclopaedia Britannica*, p. 700.

[11] Husserl, *Ideas*, p. 222.

[12] *Encyclopaedia Britannica*, p. 700b.

[13] This chapter will not explicitly dwell on Ricœur's later extentions and deepenings. Therefore, although this view of immediate understanding is later deepened, we will not follow that development here.

willing, invokes Husserl's eidetic brackets, as the "bracketing of the fact and elaborating the idea or sense," elaborating the *eidos*. However, he refuses to accept, just as Heidegger, the transcendental reduction revealing the transcendental ego as the most ultimate structure of consciousness. He considers this to be an obstacle to understanding the personal body, thus not allowing him to accept the basic incarnation theory of Marcel by which he has been guided.

On this level of his phenomenology of the will, Ricœur engages in intentional analysis and description of the essential (eidetic) structures of willing as fundamental possibilities. He considers intentionality of the will to be the center of intentionality; "I can" is presupposed by every "I think." [14] He separates these essential structures from their factual existence. Further investigation must be made to see from what Ricœur wishes to abstract in order to reach man's fundamental possibilities and the implications or basis of such an abstraction, and to justify such an abstraction. This abstraction and the abstract man it yields is fundamental to the whole of his philosophy of the will and therefore takes on great importance. This shall be done at the end of this chapter.

FUNDAMENTAL LIMIT OF EIDETIC LEVEL

The fundamental limit placed on an eidetic level of reflection on willing is obviously that of the nature of any eidetic reflection and pure description. And this eidetic reflection is Ricœur's explicit aim in *Le volontaire et l'involontaire*. As an eidetic it will "bracket the fact and elaborate the sense." (VI, 7). As pure reflection, this to some extent involves a "direct seizing of immediate experience." (DI, 443). It is an attempt at a "pure reflection," a "way of understanding and being understood which does not come through image, symbol or myth, and can reach a certain threshold of intelligibility where the possibility of evil appears inscribed in the innermost structure of human reality." (HF, 21). Ricœur on this level is trying to arrive at structures of willing, structures of man, in pure reflection. In *Le volontaire et l'involontaire* his aim is to yield the relation between the voluntary and involuntary, and their unity as a limit idea. In *L'homme faillible*, his aim is to yield by pure reflection the structures of disproportion in the synthesis of two levels in man as the existential structures making evil possible, i.e., to find the *locus* of evil in man. By placing both these investigations in the manner of an *eidetics or pure reflection,* he does not mean to imply that he does not have to go beyond the eidetic levels. Rather,

[14] Ricœur, "Philosophy of Will and Action," pp. 16-17.

he must constantly go beyond eidetics to the body and to history in order to yield the necessary structures of the involuntary correlative to those on the side of the voluntary and necessary to explain it. The attempt in going beyond the eidetics (in the first chapter of each of the three parts of VI) is to clarify that aspect of the relationship between the voluntary and the involuntary which has been grasped in the pure eidetic reflection. "It remains the task of understanding to comprehend as much as possible. This is why the relation of the corporeal involuntary to the will has to be clarified in the light of previously understood relations between motive and project." In all cases of going beyond the eidetics, the attempt is to satisfy the requirement of the stage of pure description, to clarify the relation or structure yielded by it. (VI, 129). This is a methodological prejudice of Ricœur at this level of phenomenology of will. But it is deliberate and its limitations are explicit, or he would not feel the need to carry on most of the work on this eidetic level outside the realm of the eidetics, even though for it and necessitated by it. This subordination must be kept in mind but as a methodological subordination for the sake of underlying structure.

Thus it is clear that Ricœur deliberately at this level avoids the use of representation. (VI, 82). The aim of the eidetic is to arrive at a clear understanding of the structure. Ricœur is well aware that this yields an abstract man.[15] Thus we must at the end of this chapter fully treat his arguments for this abstract man with unity which reveals the existential duality on its horizon.[16]

Principle of Reciprocity

The first product of the abstraction and pure description of the voluntary and involuntary remains to be seen. Ricœur presents the first outcome as the reciprocity between the voluntary and the involuntary, taking their unity as a limit concept. He proposes to interpret their meaning or the meaning of their unity from the top down, rather than from the bottom up, as is often the case today in this post-Freudian era. (VI, 8-9).

One of the advantages of the eidetic description was that it prevented the *Cogito* from separating itself off from corporality and then objectifying the body. It is because of this double movement of the *Cogito* that freedom and nature are first thought of as two. Understanding the one by the other struggles against this double movement. This unity is one of practical medi-

---

[15] Paul Ricœur, "Unity of the Voluntary and the Involuntary as a Limiting Idea," in *Readings in Existential Phenomenology*, ed. by Nathaniel Lawrence and Daniel O'Conner, p. 112.
[16] *Ibid.*, p. 108.

ation.[17] It is by the bracketing of fault and innocence that the primordial relation between the voluntary and the involuntary before distortion comes to light. This eidetic level of reflection as coming first in a philosophy of the will allows for the grasping of the meaning of the involuntary and of the constituting will from the constituted will.[18]

The contrast between explanation and description is Ricœur's guide in first coming to the principle of reciprocity between the voluntary and the involuntary as the first or initial situation revealed by description. Scientific explanation always moves from the complex to the simple. The method of scientific psychology leads to building up man like a house, laying a foundation with a psychology of the involuntary, and topping these initial functional levels with a supplementary level called "will." This explanation would mean that such things as need, habit, etc., all have a meaning of their own, almost a consciousness of their own, to which is added the meaning of the will, if it is not derived from them. This method does not consider the possibility that the will might be already entailed in a full understanding of the involuntary. (VI,7-8).

Description grasps this relation of the voluntary and the involuntary as a relation of reciprocal implication. Ricœur attempts to "recapture the meaning of my involuntary life as my own," before scientific consciousness makes it a realm of objects.[19] He points out that description brings to light the initial situation in which "need, emotion, habit, etc., take on a complete sense only in relation to a will which they solicit, dispose, and generally affect, and which in turn fixes their sense, that is, determines them by its choice, moves them by its effort, and adopts them by its consent." (VI, 8). Thus Ricœur, at this first stage of his phenomenology of the will, considered the involuntary not to have any meaning of its own. It is only the relation itself that is intelligible, and description understands in terms of this relation. We can also clearly see that Ricœur wishes to read the meaning from the top down, instead of vice versa, thus directly opposing himself to Freud. (VI, 8-9). This point is extremely important for the further development in later chapters, especially in relation to his confrontation with semiology in general and Freud's psychoanalysis and the deepening this confrontation necessitates in the reading of the relationship and the origin of meaning. Ricœur does not emerge unaffected from his confrontation with the challenge of semiology. However at this point of our reflection it

[17] *Ibid.,* p. 93.
[18] Paul Ricœur, "Méthode et tâches d'une phénoménologie de la volonté," in *Problèmes actuels de la phénoménologie,* ed. by H. L. van Breda, p. 121.
[19] Paul Ricœur, "The Unity of the Voluntary and the Involuntary," p. 100.

is necessary to remain within the confines of pure reflection and consider only the first steps of his philosophy of will.

The reconciliation of the voluntary and the involuntary presupposes that they confront each other in the same universe of discourse so that the voluntary cannot be treated as subjectivity while the involuntary is treated as empirical objectivity. Such a treatment requires the incarnation of the "I" with existence as body. This body is body as mine but also body as yours. By subjectivity, then, Ricœur means "the subject function of an intentional consciousness, such that I understand it as applying to me and to others"; thus it is a phenomenology of intersubjectivity.[20]

The body and the involuntary which it sustains must be discovered in the context of the *Cogito* itself. Ricœur points out that it is the same subjectivity, or a common subjectivity which is the basis for the homogeneity of the structures of the voluntary and the involuntary. These can no longer be considered as two universes of discourse, one of the *Cogito* in the realm of thought, and the other that of the body from the physical point of view. "The *Cogito's* intuition is the very intuition of the body joined to the willing which submits to it and rules over it; it is the sense of the body as the source of motives, as a cluster of capacities, and even as necessary nature." (VI, 13).

This does not mean that Ricœur tries to give a phenomenology of the involuntary. The only phenomenology he is offering here is of the reciprocity of the voluntary and the involuntary. He sees the involuntary as affecting the will as the other pole of life. The multiplicity of the involuntary is grasped only in relation to the one will. This is his guiding principle at this stage of his phenomenology allowing him to grasp the involuntary function in some order or according to some order principle. "We are thus led to decipher the involuntary-for-the-voluntary." [21] Thus Ricœur proceeds in his *Le volontaire et l'involontaire* first by an understanding and description of the voluntary and only then does he derive the understanding of the involuntary. "I understand myself first as he who says 'I will.' The involuntary refers itself to the willing as giving it motives and capacities, foundations, and even limits." (VI, 9).

Thus it is clear that such a description of the voluntary and the involuntary must be receptive to the *Cogito's* complete experience instead of letting the *Cogito* close about itself a circle and too quickly shut out its bond with the body. And he points out that we must constantly reconquer the *Cogito* grasped in the first person from the natural standpoint. (VI, 12-13).

[20] Paul Ricœur, "Unity of the Voluntary and the Involuntary," p. 101.
[21] *Ibid.,* p. 101.

Body and Subjectivity

In this manner Ricœur extends subjectivity to the body. Next, he extends subjectivity to the other. He sees these relations of motivation, motion, and necessity as intersubjective relations. (VI, 14). "A personal body is someone's body, a subject's body, my body, and your body." It is by empathy (Einfühlung) that we read the body of another as indicating acts which have a subjective aim and origin. Therefore, he concludes, subjectivity is internal and external. This view gets rid of the prejudicial identification of the subjective with the internal and is the basis of intersubjective communication.

Thus the concepts of subjectivity extended to the involuntary and to the other are formed by gathering experience from many subjects. Since he has extended the subjectivity to the other, having seen that it is not limited to myself, Ricœur can say that the concepts of subjectivity come from both directions. Knowledge of myself is a guide for knowledge of the other, and at the same time, I treat myself as a you. He thus shows how the concepts of subjectivity are formed in mutual contact of reflection and introspection. (VI, 15). Thus the transition to the naturalistic viewpoint from the phenomenological takes place by the degradation of both the internal and the external instead of by inversion of them. (VI, 15).

Diagnostics

It is the same body that is both subject and object. It appears as the body of a subject and at the same time as the empirical object. The object body is one among many objects and is considered in relation to them. As such it is considered to be a whole, among other wholes in a system of objects. The experienced body, however, is or corresponds to a behavior of the will, and is thus an abstracted part, set apart from the subject as a whole. Thus we cannot simply consider the scientific attitude and the phenomenological attitude as two points of view. (VI, 15).

It is the breakdown of uniform activity in the view of the body as an empirical object which makes us change perspectives or point of view in attempting to express the subjective experience of freedom. The dependence of the body on the self which governs it, uses it, consents to it, wills in and through it, has no counterpart in the universe of discourse of the empirical science which deals with it as a body or object among others governed by laws in a system, viewed from the natural standpoint. (VI, 15). Thus, the experience of the effort to exist is inexplicable to empirical knowledge and must be reduced by it. Its explication as a fact and as some kind of force is in the final analysis *a breakdown in uniform objectivity*. (VI, 15). This difficulty was realized by Kant in his practical reason, so that for him it becomes necessary to invoke the noumenal realm or aspect to explain freedom, and to see freedom as constitutive.

But these different viewpoints do not mean that there is not a relation between the lived body which is mine or yours, and the body of the empirical science. Since they are actually the same body there must be a relation.

It is the insight into this correlation that allows Ricœur in descriptive analysis the diagnostic use of the strict and empirical sciences to help arrive at the conception of the structures of the voluntary and the involuntary. This diagnostic use of empirical science is similar to the doctor's use of symptoms to diagnose the trouble of the patient. From certain descriptions in the empirical sciences, Ricœur tries to make explicit the implicit phenomenology contained in them and come to these structures. Since it is the same body that is being discussed in his pure description and in these empirical sciences, he can use the latter to arrive at the essential structures of the voluntary and the involuntary. (VI, 16). This diagnostic use of science transcends the pure form of Husserlian phenomenology. It calls for a releasing of the more close abstraction or reduction after each part of pure description in the essential moments of the willing and its correlates.

This analysis of the transcending of the descriptive analysis by a dialectics does not sufficiently explain why in Ricœur's further analysis his initial description of the forms of willing requires in each case a deepening in the direction of more essential connections. "The bond which joins the willing to its body requires another type of attention other than the intellectual attention to structures." I must go further by actively participating in my incarnation as mystery and pass from objectivity to existence. (VI, 17-18).

For this descriptive analysis of the reciprocity of the voluntary and the involuntary, it is not sufficient to grasp the extension of the *Cogito* to the personal body. We must also see as Ricœur does, the further meaning of objectivity for phenomenology. (VI, 17-18). This is no longer the objectivity of naturalism or of the thing. It is the objectivity on a higher order of concepts of the voluntary and the involuntary and of the concepts of the *Cogito*. It might be called objective in the sense that it poses various essences before thought as it objects, such as perceiving, imagining, or willing (in *noematic* analysis). This type of thought in respecting what presents itself as *Cogito* is phenomenology and description. (VI, 18-19). Yet even though this is not a naturalistic objectivity, it entails a definite loss of being, and is a cutting off from the presence of reality. If we heed the presence of the body, we can not suspend the existence of a "world prolonging that of my body as its horizon." (VI, 20).

Ricœur is of the opinion that if the suspension of the existence of the world as the horizon of the body is allowed, the *Cogito*, in losing the existence of the world also loses the existence of its body and finally its marks as a first person. Therefore, the philosophy of man appears to him as a "living tension between an objectivity elaborated by a phenomenology proportionate to the *Cogito* . . . and the sense of my incarnate existence." (VI, 20). This latter realm of existence exceeds that of the former objectivity and overflows it. Thus the concepts used, as project, motivation, situation, are "indications of a living experience in which we are submerged more than signs of mastery which our intelligence exercises over our human condition." (VI, 17). The function of his descriptive phenomenology, therefore, is to clarify existence by the use of such concepts.

But this living bond must be constantly reconquered. (VI, 22). Within the experienced unity there is a new dualism, a dualism of existence. Existence tends to break itself up. Each of the moments of the willing expresses this dualism. This will can be seen when Ricœur returns to its further elaboration in order to render the existential conditions of man on the ethical level.

Failure of Unity and Existential Split

It is the failure of the unity of the voluntary and the involuntary which leads to the existential split or rift which marks the transition for Ricœur from *Le volontaire et l'involontaire* to *L'homme faillible*. We see in the failure of this unity the posing of a limit idea. He has attempted to oppose the dualism of the understanding (VI), but the duality of existence has arisen as founding the duality of understanding, and this failure of unity leads to the notion of a limit idea.

In the eidetics of the will, as long as the endeavor is to simply articulate the meanings of the will and desire, acting and ability to act, of consenting and necessity, then the unity of the voluntary and the involuntary holds up. But as soon as the effort is made to elaborate an existential synthesis, "as soon as one tries to get closer to the concrete life of consciousness, to the existential development of an individual," the failure of the unity becomes manifest.[22]

Receptivity of the Voluntary

Ricœur considers motivation to be the receptive moment of decision. I

[22] Paul Ricœur, "The Unity of the Voluntary and the Involuntary," p. 105.

decide this because ... motivation is this relation of the will to an intentional stream inclining it. This body, this desire in some way nourishes
motivation. The need is represented by the imagination taken as a manner
of anticipating an absent reality, and this imagination can mediate between
need and will. But desire then is the image-making anticipation of pleasure
itself and not just of the absent thing.[23] This already affective imagination
is a pre-reflective apprehension of value. However, by means of the anticipated pleasure, I believe in the "goodness" of the bread without affirming
or judging it. For Ricœur, this is the affective anticipation of good and of
evil.[24] Thus, he has shown how the most elementary need illustrates the
coming together of the two lines of analysis. The will in its most receptive
moments is open to the suggestions of the involuntary. Human affectivity
as an established lack and anticipation of satisfaction is transfigured by an
evaluative intention raising the body to the level of a field of motivation.[25]
Thus even before arising to discourse (*logos*) our body transcends itself to
become body of a man, the body of a self that wills.

In this first main moment of willing, deciding, Ricœur has illustrated the
unity of the voluntary and the involuntary and the receptivity of the voluntary. It is necessary to outline the other two main moments in their receptivity to the involuntary before seeing how and why this unity finally
fails and must be held in view as a regulative idea guiding the further development.

Desire is taken up by the will or comes up to meet it also in action in
which it serves as nascent action or the power which the body offers to
voluntary action. Ricœur insists on "two properly human forms of involuntary action," emotion and habit, which help to recover the meaning of the
body as acting, as an unreflective use of our body.

The naturalistic explanation which obliterates the involuntary meaning
of emotion can be turned around, so that the incoherent disorders still have
a meaning, typical of the fragile order of man, which is still a disorder of
man.

Habit also has this specific human quality and cannot be reduced simply
to an automatism. In the body's offering itself as a practical mediation,
habit co-ordinates and facilitates action, as in familiar gestures, while not

[23] Paul Ricœur, "The Unity of the Voluntary and the Involuntary," p. 104.
[24] *Ibid.*, p. 102.
[25] We shall see in the later chapters of this work that Ricœur modifies this view.
For he learns from Freud that the body and desire are already human, already have
a meaning, and it is this meaning, at first hidden, which comes to the representation.
However, it is necessary to wait until later in the development of this treatment to
explicitly focus on this deepening in his view.

losing the aspect of spontaneity. Thus the meaning of the body is to make itself a human body, opening itself for practical use toward the world in accordance with voluntary intentions of a man.

The next step for Ricœur is to rediscover the "stamp of subjectivity in necessity: my character, my unconscious, my life." [26] This subjectivity comes to light precisely in the exercise of my power where I take unawares the provisions of nature from which they break away. In dwelling on this subjectivity of necessity, Ricœur finds the difficulty of the problematical self. He comes to a "constituted partiality of the concrete constituting self which I am," [27] bringing man's finitude to light.

Remaining consistent to his original effort to fathom the depths of the *Cogito's* full experiences, Ricœur now brings to light the full extension of the subjectivity or "my ownness" of the body, of the narrowness of finitude's openness. He indicates the subjectivity's inherence in character, in the Freudian unconscious, and even in my life-situation. This last is the extreme hold of nature on me, with its necessity, manifesting my existence as a state. Here, he is able to bring together my existence as a state with its subjective necessity and my act of existing. In this context, "*Cogito ergo sum*," reinterpreted, means, by a practical mediation, the consenting will is bound to its situation. Existence comes to light as both endured and willed.

Thus we see that the very project of *Le volontaire et l'involontaire* is to bring out this intentional unity of the voluntary and the involuntary in their reciprocity. However, it reaches the limit of a continual deepening of method (cf VI, 7-19) so that an existential duality must be admitted. All three moments of willing and of freedom itself can be seen and interpreted from two points of view. Each moment has its aspect of receptivity. This receptivity will be seen as the *locus* of a changed emphasis after his *La symbolique du mal* and after his later confrontation with Freud and semiology.

This failure of unity gives rise for Ricœur to the notion of a limiting idea in much the same fashion as the Kantian regulative ideas. However, he wishes to extend the use of regulative ideas beyond the Kantian foundations of scientific knowledge. What he proposes is a human ideal, a meaning for human unity which is the idea of motivated, incarnate, contingent freedom.[28]

It seems that the unity arrived at by Heidegger in terms of care and

[26] Paul Ricœur, "The Unity of the Voluntary and the Involuntary," p. 104.
[27] *Ibid.,* p. 104.
[28] *Ibid.,* p. 107.

temporality is comparable to this unity which Ricœur hesitates to affirm here, and for which he criticizes Heidegger's quick arrival. (CI, 27) For Ricœur, we can decipher this unity from myths and stories [29] in which its experiences are manifest, or we can take it as a limit concept or as a task; but we must not too quickly affirm it ontologically as men's mode of being, identifying unity with an a priori structure as achieved already rather than as a sight to be won.

Essential Nature of Man and Abstraction as Eidetic Limit

Ricœur is quick to point out that his presentation within the eidetics is that of an abstract man. He wishes to emphasize that he is presenting the essential nature of man and not his empirical conditions, nor simply his factual being. He attempts to avoid the possibility of coming up with a man whose being is misunderstood because of the distortion in its everyday appearance and manifestation due to misleading accidentals which distort the pure view of man's nature. In its most general terms, the eidetics wishes to treat the "abstract man" in his essential structures as man, leaving out of consideration the variations. Fault and innocence are modalities of man's being which can be considered as variations of his one essential nature, as both played out on the "undifferentiated keyboard" (HF, 10) of innocence and guilt.

This broader view of the possibilities of eidetics extended to the very nature of man, as his undifferentiated and invariable structures, no matter what the particular modalities of his accidental and concrete existence which remain the same in all manifestations, is the theme that is basic to the whole of his philosophy of the will. This theme then brings out the contrast between the different stages in which he considers man from different perspectives. When he releases what he has bracketed in the eidetics and pure reflection, Ricœur will consider man in the concrete. But from the start the first level is seen to underlie all the others so that it must be elaborated first as a guide to the other levels of his philosophy of the will.

Since the full significance of the fundamental structures of the voluntary and the involuntary are not understood until this limiting abstraction is removed, Ricœur realizes the necessity to justify at the outset such an abstraction. Although pure description and pure understanding of the willing, voluntary and involuntary, are constituted by this bracketing of fault and transcendence, which bracketing alters the intelligibility of their relation,

[29] Paul Ricœur, "The Unity of the Voluntary and the Involuntary," p. 108.

the advantages of this perspective are partial justification of it. By bracketing the fault, we are allowed to grasp this primitive relation before its distortion, in the essential structures of man. Although *pure understanding* abstracts from fault and innocence, it does so in order to more fully understand them in its more full return to them later, in deeper considerations, with a different method.

Ricœur speaks of this abstraction first as an abstraction of the passions. This must be clarified. In such an abstraction he in no way means to disassociate the passions from the will. In fact, he asserts that they are not only not alien to the will, but rather are the will itself, in its everyday, concrete, real aspect. This is precisely why the abstraction from fault and passions must be justified. (VI, 23). In doing this it shall become clear how the method of abstraction is the means of posing the problem correctly, of showing that servitude and deliverance happen to freedom. (VI, 36) It shall also become clear that the method of abstraction is for him the occasion for surpassing and deepening that "I" which is always on the point of closing in on itself. It is now necessary to turn to the treatment of objections to this abstraction. (VI, 23-36)

Abstraction from Passion

Passion must not be considered a part of man nor to deal only with the involuntary. Passion is a distortion of both the voluntary and the involuntary, of the finite and of the infinite. Passions proceed from the region of the will itself. In the sense that the spell of passion comes from the soul, the passions are the will itself, but find their temptation and means in the involuntary. "They seize the human totality by the head and make it an alienated totality." (VI, 24) Therefore, each passion can be considered the form of the human totality.

An abstraction from passion is also an abstraction from the law, since real, concrete understanding of morality begins with the passions. The values for the choice of the will become obligatory after the manner of a hard law in reference to the passions. "In perverting the involuntary and the voluntary, the fault alters our fundamental relation to values and opens the true drama of the moral which is the drama of divided man." (VI, 24)

There are several traits of passion that need to be borne out more explicitly. First of all, the principle of passion is a certain bondage, but one which the soul imposes on itself. However, the bondage is neither the necessity of nature or determinism, nor that of the involuntary. It is a bondage to nothing. The nothing projected draws the soul into an endless pursuit and begins the "bad infinite" of passion. Lastly, the fault is an

alien body in the essential structures of man. It is not an element of fundamental ontology on the same level as the other factors discovered by pure
description, such as motive, powers, conditions. Rather the fault is absurd.
(HF, 10) This manifests Ricœur's strong conviction in the eidetics and pure
reflection against the ontologizing of fault and guilt, which results from
too quickly going to ontology, and to some extent, indicates the need to
justify his methodological conviction of the need for an indirect access to
such characteristics on the empirical and concrete level of man's existence.

This last aspect of the fault, that it is not homogeneous with the other
elements yielded by the descriptive method, demands most convincingly
that fault be set aside. The main strength of this methodical reason is that
there cannot be an eidetic description beginning with an accident but only
an empirical one. (VI, 24) In order to decipher the passions, we must
study man through the usages of life and ordinary discourse.

But the abstraction of the passions is necessary in order to arrive at the
authentic infinite instead of getting fixed in the bad infinite, to make
freedom available to us, and to see the bonds which join even necessity to
freedom.

In discussing the possibility and necessity of abstracting the fault and
the passions Ricœur proceeds by answering several objections, thereby
illuminating some essential aspects of his procedure and justifying the abstraction. (VI, 28-31)

1. To the first objection that an abstraction from such an important
dimension of human reality is impossible, Ricœur replies by pointing out
that an eidetic description can take even an imaginary or an imperfect,
truncated, distorted experience. Since the fault does not destroy the fundamental structure, such an abstraction does not destroy the essential structures which as a whole fall into the power of Nothing.

2. To the objection that the eidetic pretends to describe an innocent
existence which is not accessible to us, Ricœur answers that it is not accu-
rate to say that we are attempting to describe the structure of innocence
but rather that we are trying to describe the structures that underlie both
innocence and fault. What is to be described in the eidetics are the structures which are the fundamental possibilities of both. As a matter of fact,
innocence is not accessible to any description, eidetic or empirical, but
rather only to a mythics, and itself serves as the setting for any empirical
description of the fault and the passions considered as a lost innocence or
lost paradise.

3. The next objection proposes that corruption seizes the whole man,
both the voluntary and the involuntary, rendering consideration of possi-

bilities apart from innocence or fault impossible. Would they not be neutral? Also, are we not separating the depth of human nature from a superficial fault or innocence? Ricœur answers by asserting that we must understand that a fundamental nature subsists even within the most complete fault. "The fault ends up in freedom; the guilty will is a servile freedom and not a return to an animal or mineral nature from which freedom would be absent." (VI, 29) For Ricœur, the reason it is possible to abstract the fault is that the "empirical truth of man as slave is added to the eidetic truth of man as free." (VI, 29)

4. The last objection presents this difficulty, that if fault seizes man as a whole, there is a risk of bringing into the description traits that belong to freedom in bondage. Is it possible that freedom is understood only by beginning with the fall? Perhaps the only type of freedom is that in bondage. Ricœur sees this as the movement of Kierkegaard's analysis of fault, moving from the fault as a fall to the fault as the source of increase in consciousness of freedom.

In answer to this last objection, Ricœur opposes himself to the movement begun by Kierkegaard developed by Jaspers, and achieved by Heidegger. He thinks that only by a pure description of the voluntary and the involuntary abstracting from the fault can the fault be revealed as a fall, a loss, an absurdity, that is, bring out its negative force in full. Ricœur sees this pure description as providing a setting, a limit, for a fundamental ontology, which prohibits us from making the knowledge of the fault, the passions, and of the law into an ontology. The phenomenon of the fault hides the being of the human condition, making it unavailable. But the "being of freedom is limiting only because it is constitutive." (VI, 30)

Abstraction of Transcendence

Since the abstraction of the fault and of transcendence are inseparable, one implies the other, and therefore the abstraction of transcendence is necessary. The experience of fault and the mythical vision of innocence are closely linked with an affirmation of transcendence. Transcendence is what liberates freedom from the fault. Men live transcendence as purification and deliverance of their freedom as salvation. The myth of innocence involves the beginning and the end, the genesis and the eschatology.

We have seen how pure description leads to pure understanding of the intelligibility of the voluntary and involuntary in the unity and disproportion of this relation; how this is aligned with Husserl of the period of *Logic* and *Ideas,* instead of going straight to the *Lebenswelt* period, and how description demands abstraction from fault and transcendence to bring to light the neutral structure of the will.

In his defense of this abstraction from the accidental condition or characteristics of man to reach an eidetic or abstract man in his essential structures, it becomes clear what Ricœur means in criticizing contemporary existential phenomenologists for going too quickly to the *Lebenswelt* period of Husserl's phenomenology. However, this abstraction also prevents the "I" from closing in on itself and allows for its deepening, (VI, 36), in the fashion of Marcel's incarnation theory. It thus prevents the "I" from abstracting itself or from separating itself from the bodily and involuntary, and then objectifying these in the manner of the natural or naturalistic attitude.

But at the same time, the abstraction is admittedly a limitation. It is only later, in the releasing of the abstraction, that the fuller understanding of man and his structures can be grasped. However, the abstraction supplies the guiding themes and a limit for fundamental ontology. Without such a limit, there is danger of existential monism, of ontologizing fault and many other aspects of man's empirical existence. Ricœur thus with a beginning in eidetics clears the way for the Being of the human condition, for a fuller grasp of fundamental ontology. This becomes clear from the fundamental principle yielded by this pure description, from the polemical unity of man as a regulative idea.

CHAPTER III

EXISTENTIAL STRUCTURES OF DISPROPORTION

In order to reach essential structures and relationships of structures, abstracting from the concrete and variable is necessary. For Ricœur, the descent into the consideration of concrete man or concrete reflection is a gradual one achieved in steps. Before the passage to concrete reflection he saw the further need for *L'homme faillible,* which concerns the existential structures of disproportion as the *locus* of evil in man. He is preoccupied with the question of disproportion and synthesis (HF). It is not simply a question of the synthesis of the objectivity of the object in the subjectivity of the subject for strictly theoretical knowledge in the style of Kant. For Ricœur it is fundamentally a question of the unity of man and especially of his practical and affective synthesis. He extends his perspective as broadly as possible to consider a global view of man, taking the transcendental method as his guideline. From the guidance of this transcendental level he renders problematical the totality of man and extends the method, even on the object, to practical antinomies and their synthesis and then to the affective poles and synthesis.

Dealing with the eidetic structures of disproportion on these different levels of synthesis, Ricœur does not release the bracketing of fault. At the outset he indicates in the introduction and in other writings on this level, the source or *locus* of this possibility in fallibility, in disproportion. But he wishes to consider this fallibility of man as not identified with his finitude, and to grasp man's fallibility from a global view on man. He starts with a transcendental reflection limited by its one point of view and rendering the totality problematical.

TWOFOLD HYPOTHESIS

Ricœur begins the discussion in this work by proposing what he calls a double hypothesis or twofold interest of reason,[1] one phase dealing with doctrine and the other with method.

Methodological: The first working hypothesis basically is that the idea or concept of fallibility is one that is accessible to pure reflection and designates an ontological aspect of man's being. By accessible to pure reflection he means accessible to a way "of understanding and of being understood which does not proceed by image, symbol, or myth. . . ." (MF, 21) Our discussion will focus mainly on the methodological hypothesis or presupposition and its transitions.

Doctrinal: The second part of the working hypothesis is one of doctrine. According to it, the ground or basis of the concept of man's fallibility is a certain "non-coincidence of man with himself," (HF, 21) a disproportion of self to self as the *ratio* of fallibility. For Ricœur this presents to us the constitutive weakness of man by which evil is rendered possible. It is the pure possibility of man's doing evil, or of his falling and therefore of fault. This disproportion in man as the tension between the polarity of the finite and the infinite demands that in man there be a mediation or a mediating function. It is essential to understand that this mediating function is not exterior, as with Descartes, who views man as midway between being and nothing. Rather, this mediation is man himself in the sense that it is within him. He mediates "things" in their synthesis, and he mediates his activities and his feelings. "He is intermediary because he is mixed and he is mixed because he brings about mediations." (HF, 23)

One cannot begin with one aspect of this antinomy of limited and unlimited, of finite and infinite, but with the antinomy itself. Thus Kant's categories of quality, reinterpreted or reapplied, will be arrived at. In this hypothesis, Ricœur questions and disagrees with taking finitude as the central concept of philosophical anthropology. In looking for fallibility in disproportion, the question of where to begin arises. He wants to begin with the composite itself, from the relation finite-infinite, with the whole man, i.e., the global view of the noncoincidence with himself, his disproportion and the mediating function in existing. (HF, 24) But the difficulty is the possibility that such a moving within the totality could result with no order, no logical sequence, no progression. Therefore he proposes the possibility of a series of viewpoints or approaches which would each, in turn, be a viewpoint on the totality. (HF, 24)

The essential concern here is the important distinction Ricœur makes between method in philosophy and a starting point from which philosophi-

[1] Paul Ricœur, "The Antinomy of Human Reality and the Problem of Philosophical Anthropology," in *Readings in Existential Phenomenology,* p. 391.

cal anthropology might begin its reflection on disproportion. This starting point is not philosophical, but pre-philosophical, and is a precomprehension of the disproportion, which the philosophical discussion must elucidate.

Everything which the philosopher could say in clear terms has already been said enigmatically, pre-philosophically, in the complete language of myth and symbol.[2] The totality has been given in some way prior to philosophical reflection. In other words, philosophy and method of philosophy begin with what is already pre-philosophically understood prior to reflection.

For Ricœur, such a precomprehension of fallible man is found in the *pathétique* of misery. His first endeavor is to find some excellent expressions of this *pathétique* which would reveal man's precomprehension of himself as miserable because of the disproportion within him. He finds this in Plato, in Pascal, and in Kierkegaard.

TRANSCENDENTAL REFLECTION

In making the transition from the *pathétique* to philosophical anthropology, a reflection of a transcendental style is used. This is a reflection which begins with the object before me being traced back to its conditions of possibility, or the synthesis in the object. (HF, 25) Such a philosophical reflection must begin by bracketing the *pathétique,* the pre-philosophical, to reach a philosophical transcendental stage or level. However, such a reflection does not exhaust what the *pathétique* offers for reflection. "The transcendental only furnishes the first moment of a philosophical anthropology and does not equal everything of which the *pathétique* of misery is the pre-comprehension." (HF, 25) This is precisely the crux of Ricœur's endeavor to extend the transcendental mode of reflection or, in other words, to supplement it with a pure reflection that goes beyond the limits of the transcendental style in the strict sense. His attempt is to recover progressively the *pathétique* of misery by pure reflection. The transcendental reflection serves as the guide for this whole book, and in a way for all that follows in the next. "The whole movement of this book consists in an effort to gradually enlarge reflection. . . ." (HF, 26) However, *pure reflection* never attains total comprehension of the *pathétique* of misery in man's precomprehension of himself, "because there is in the precomprehension of man by himself a richness of sense which is not equalled by reflection." (HF, 26) It is precisely this residue of meaning which causes Ricœur to turn to a different approach in the next section of this volume

---

[2] Paul Ricœur, "The Antinomy of Human Reality," p. 391.

(SM). As we shall see further on, the method is called for here in this problematics . . . "no longer by pure reflection, but by an exegesis of the fundamental symbols in which man makes the avowal of the servitude of his free will." (HF, 26)

Advantages of the transcendental

1. The strength of the transcendental reflection lies first in its choice of a beginning. (HF, 35) It begins by an examination of the power of knowing. This is a choice to situate all of man's characteristics with reference to the one which a critique of knowledge brings into focus. As far as Ricœur is concerned, by such a beginning, the question of doing and feeling are thus placed in a specific light which is suitable for a reflection on man. The categories of both the above realms would not be suitable for philosophical anthropology if not first subjected to the critical test of transcendental reflection. (HF, 35-36) This choice of a point of departure concerns us because the first disproportion for a philosophical investigation is brought into view from the power of knowing. This brings into view the transcendental imagination as the third term for Kant's reflection on the faculties of man's knowing, the intermediary between the understanding and sensibility.

2. In elucidating the reason such a beginning and reflection on the transcendental imagination in a Kantian style concerns a philosophy of fallibility, Ricœur points out another strength for beginning here in the transcendental style of reflection. This is a type of reflection that does not begin with the self and so is not introspection but reflection. It begins with the object or the thing. It is upon the thing that the reflection discovers the disproportion of knowing between receiving it and determining it, and apprehends the power of synthesis. This transcendental reflection is not immediate consciousness of the self, but takes the detour in the roundabout way of the object. It is a reflection on the object. (HF, 36) It is transcendental because it starts with the object and attempts to discover the conditions of the possibility of the synthesis of the object or on the object. This is a break from the *pathétique*. The problem of disproportion is now brought up to the philosophical dimension. (HF, 36)

However, the strength itself reveals the very limitation of this reflection. Its limitation is precisely this, that it remains necessary to pass from such a consciousness to self-consciousness. This is the case because the synthesis it brings to light is in the object, in the thing, merely intentional and therefore projected outside into the world, into the structure of the objectivity it makes possible. (HF, 36) Therefore, the problem Ricœur is considering and bringing to light is precisely this, that while this is a synthesis, as a consciousness bringing synthesis only to the object outside, and rendering such objectivity possible, it does not speak of the synthesis of the self or the overcoming of the disproportion wrought in the self as revealed by the *pathétique*. A style of mediation other than the transcendental style is necessary to continue it and pass from consciousness to self-consciousness.

This mediation will be one of pure reflection which, in taking up the practical, marks the passage from the theoretical to the practical, from a theory of knowledge to a theory of the will. This new venture of reflection answers the need for totality. We have already seen how the transcendental reflection has its strength in breaking with the *pathétique* and thus opens up the philosophical dimension of an anthropology; and how it has its limitation in the same, i.e., that it begins with the thing, to reflect on the "conditions of the possibility of the objectivity of the thing." (HF, 64) This is its limitation because the universe of things is still only the *abstract framework* of our life-world. This means that the constituting of a world still lacks all the affective and practical aspects, the values and counter-values, the means, tools, instruments which make this world practicable or impracticable and difficult. (HF, 65) It especially lacks the presence of persons "with whom we work, fight and communicate and who rise out of that horizon of things, on the decor of pragmatic and valorized objects, as other poles of subjectivity, apprehension, valorization and action." (HF, 65)

3. It is first in the object that we discern the gap between a transcendental consideration and a totalizing consideration. This is because the "world of persons expresses itself across the world of things, in filling this world of things with new things which are human works." (HF, 65) By beginning with the pure thing, and reflecting on the pure concepts, the pure receiving and the pure imagination, the total person has become problematical, and there is an awareness of completing this partial abstract view. This for Ricœur is such a consideration because it has rendered problematical the question of totality and thereby made it philosophical.

4. Another advantage of such a procedure is that this transcendental reflection not only shows the totality as a problem but also as a term of approximation in the sense that it must be approached by degrees and not all at once. (HF, 65-66) For Ricœur, the theory of the will constitutes the principal stage between the "pure" of transcendental and the "total," "the point of bending the abstract into the concrete." (HF, 66) This can not be the last stage, as the stage of the feelings will make clear.

5. Another advantage of beginning with a transcendental reflection is that this manner of reflection is already on the primordial level and does not treat sensibility as already fallen. This is the main reason Ricœur takes it as guide. It does not begin with radical evil, with ethical duality, but on the contrary, reaches to disproportion underlying fallen, accidental conditions. (HF, 95)

6. A final advantage which Ricœur says can be drawn from the transcendental reflection is that it will illuminate and orientate the approach to the human totality by supplying it with the triad – perspective, meaning, and synthesis, which becomes the "melodic germ of all the subsequent developments." (HF, 66) In this new stage of reflection, the person and not the thing is the object which serves as guide. The poles of the tension carried down to this level are character, happiness, and the practical mediation as the constitution of the person by means of respect, which corresponds with and carries down the transcendental imaginations. (HF, 66-67)

TRANSCENDENTAL REFLECTION AND ITS EXTENSION

This discussion is concerned with Ricœur's development as it closes the gap between the transcendental and the *pathétique*. The first extension of the transcendental style of reflection springing from its inherent limitation can be seen even from the object as was discussed in treating the second advantage of transcendental reflection. The second reason for the insufficiency of this mode of reflection comes from the nature of the unity to which it gives rise, a synthesis that is only intentional and formal. Therefore, thirdly, it is the form of the world in theoretical knowledge for consciousness, but is not that of self consciousness or the unity of self.

Ricœur's extension of this reflection to the practical and to the affective begins with his disagreement with Kant on the nature of the epistemological synthesis of the object. He does not limit it to the synthesis that is strictly scientific, preferring to call it objectival rather than objective or objectivity. (HF, 56) He does not place the thing's a priori synthesis in the first principles. Rather than in this objectival character, he places it in the property of being thrown before me (intentionality), given to my point of view, and able to be communicated in a language. "That is the objectivity of the object, that the expressibility adheres to the appearance of whatever it may be." (HF, 56) This objectivity for Ricœur is the thing's mode of being. Ricœur explicitly admits an agreement with Heidegger in indicating that the Copernican revolution is first a return "from the ontic to the ontological constitution," (HF, 57) as a synthetic constitution, a uniting of meaning to presence.

What makes this reflection transcendental instead of psychological is that the thing's ontological constitution, its objectivity, is a guide to coming to awareness of the subjective synthesis. It is necessary here only to see the need to extend beyond the transcendental mode of reflection with the reasons for this extension.

From the above discussion, it is clear what Ricœur means when he indicates that as only an intentional unity projected on the object. This arises from his difference with the Kantian interpretation or initiation of the mode of reflection which is specifically transcendental, and from rendering a more Husserlian interpretation to transcendental. The synthesis is on the object and not in the self or of the self. Although it is an intentional unity, Ricœur points out that "I make myself a synthesis of speech and perspective in this projection of objectivity." (HF, 57)

Thus this unity is merely intentional and formal; intentional "since it is exhausted in the unity of the object; merely formal, since it is anterior to all content." [3] The "I" of the "I think" is the form of a world for all men. It is consciousness in general.[4]

It has become clear that the specific need giving rise to this extension of reflection is one of totality. Ricœur has throughout this phase of his reflection been taken up with the global view or vision of man, especially as yielded in the prephilosophical rhetoric or myths. (HF, 64) Thus the need to go beyond a merely transcendental consideration has been made clear. This concern for the totality has brought Ricœur from a theory of knowledge to a theory of the will. The transcendental mode of reflection has yielded only an abstract world lacking the affective and practical aspects, values, and obstacles, all the ways, tools, and instruments. But especially, it lacks the presence of persons with whom we live, work, have a world and communicate. For Ricœur, ". . . this world of persons expresses itself across the world of things by peopling it with new things which are human works." (HF, 65)

This totality of human reality or the idea of totality is a directive idea in the Kantian sense as a demand. It shall be approached gradually, step by step. This stage for Ricœur is the principal stage between the abstract and the concrete and of the descent into the concrete. It thus takes on primordial importance in the development toward the concrete man and concrete reflection of his existential condition. (HF, 675) But this is not the last stage.

Ricœur sees on this level the disproportion of man's finitude and in-

[3] Paul Ricœur, "The Antinomy of Human Reality," p. 396.
[4] *Ibid.*, p. 396.

finitudes as between character and happiness, which are synthesized by respect.

Following the guidelines of the transcendental reflection, he sees the practical mediation in respect, carrying down the mediation of the transcendental imagination, character as all the aspects of practical finitude and happiness as summarizing all the aspects of practical infinitude. (HF, 67)

But this synthesis of humanity in myself or in another is still on the object instead of within myself. It is not already achieved, but rather must be seen as a task to be brought about, "and this task is what we call the idea of the person." [5] Ricœur attributes it to Kant to have grasped that the person is a task rather than a reality.

Human fallibility in disproportion reaches its most intensity in feeling. Feeling is both intentional and affective. It projects out and so can have an intentional analysis starting with the object. But feeling also touches the depth of the person, of the self, and is the deepest point of disproportion, since it is the most intimate point of the person.[6]

Ricœur gives affective fragility the primary place in fallibility because of its function in the constitution of the person. This function is the inverse of the function of "objectivication." Instead of projecting in front of us, feeling functions to reincorporate into the vital depths what has thus been removed from the depths of life, a movement of interiorization.[7] Thus the disproportion is brought home to me into my depth. The disproportion in fragility is intimate, within my innermost being. The synthesis on this level is a fragile one.

Using the transcendental guideline set forth in the beginning of this, Ricœur investigates practical and affective Fragility.

PURE REFLECTION ON THE PRACTICAL

After considering the transcendental beginning and the need to extend pure reflection to the practical and the affective synthesis, these two latter realms must be discussed more fully. This will illuminate not only the extension of method reaching the existential, but will elucidate at this early stage of his philosophy of will problems and reasons for Ricœur's turn to experience expressed in symbols and myths.

[5] Paul Ricœur, "The Antinomy of Human Reality," p. 398.
[6] *Ibid.*, p. 399.
[7] *Ibid.*, p. 399.

Character

Ricœur wishes to move gradually from theoretical finitude in perspective or point of view to the practical finitude or character. Character adds the totality of the diverse aspects of finitude, the generalization of the notion of perspective, the unique manner of an individual's exercise of freedom. In approaching character gradually, the first stage of the approach is to add the affective aspect to the neutralized or disinterested perspective of the theoretical consideration, and then to add the practical aspects.

Affective perspective

In considering the affective aspects of perspective, Ricœur begins in much the same way as with the theoretical order, with the openness first, and then with perspective as the closing of openness. Thus it is clear that affective perspective is not what first comes to light. On the contrary, it is the thing which first emerges, the thing on which affections are aimed or projected. These affective aspects of the things motivate in the practical life and nourish the will. "It is by nourishing with motives a will which projects or is projected that my affective life unfolds its spontaneous or reflective evaluations." (HF, 68) Thus, what is first turned to is what *is being* done, and this comes into the *pragma,* the what *is to be done.* Thus the affective rootedness of the will comes to light, as Aristotle said, "The will moves through desire." (HF, 78)

Commenting on the text, Ricœur indicates that action of the will is first the movement by which I posit my acts, and is pre-reflective in the sense that it is not first a movement of attributing my acts to myself. The first act is in the intentional movement through which I have before me the "pragma." I am initially turned to the object of my project.[8] Thus, for Ricœur, the determining of self in deciding, the attribution to the self of acts, is not the first and fundamental act of willing.

Motivation indicates a specific "practical receptivity" for a project, described as an "inclination." This inclination is the specific "passion" of the will. The will must be aroused, inclined, then it determines itself. "Its activity is imbued with this specific passivity." (p. 69)

Just as in the analysis of the theoretical, the openness of the perceptual preceded its limitation or closure and perspective, so it is with desire. Openness to all the affective tones of things which attract and repel me precedes closure. The attraction or repulsion of the thing is what makes

[8] Ricœur treats this more fully in VI, p. 42. In fact, treatment in HF simply summarises and repeats the former.

for openness. Ricœur considers desire in a manner parallel to his treatment of opening and closing in perception and meaning: the vision of the world in perception, the openness then the closing.

Reflection moves from the desirable on the world to the desiring body, just as it went from the perceiving body to the projecting body. And just as perception has its finitude in the perspective, the zero point of origin in the body, so desire's finitude comes to light here, as the confusion darkening the clarity of desire. This takes the intentionality of desire as its clarity. (HF, 71)

Taking intentionality of desire as its clarity, Ricœur holds that its intentionality is elucidated by "the light of its representation." (HF, 71) Desire elucidates its intentionality, its aim, through a pre-grasping in anticipation, in the representation of the desired thing, of the means and obstacles of its attainment. These representations elucidate desire's intentionality to the world and direct desire to the world. In them "I am out of myself" (HF, 83) In bringing desire to its good, the image informs desire and this is desire itself. "Through it (the image) desire enters into the field of motivation" (HF, 71) and can be compared with other motives from the point of view of value.

Thus its affective aim is the clarity of desire. However, although desire is clear in its images, it is at the same time confused. There is a confusion or closing that does not pass into the image. Ricœur here indicates what he calls the other side of the intentionality of desire as that which does not aim, i.e., it is "the manner in which one finds oneself." (HF, 72) It is a turning back of my body into itself, "no longer a mediator, but feeling itself. Coenesthesis is precisely this." (HF, 84) Thus the body is not just openness, but beneath the openness there is this "feeling."

He now proceeds to close the gap, showing how affective point of view is self-love. First, the affective closing, the finding oneself in a certain mood, makes my fundamental difference between the I and all others arise, which in turn leads to a preference – self-preference. Ricœur attaches this to inclination as the self-attachment of all inclination. This self-love is the affective unity of all affective aims. This becomes more manifest if one's life as a whole is threatened, when the multiplicity of desirables comes back to this self-love as first desirable, turning now into the will-to-live rather than self-love. (HF, 72-73)

Practical perspective

This closing also is in the powers which serve the will. This time, the body comes to the fore as the organ and in this function it is traversed in action.

(HF, 86) In encountering a resistance the body comes to the fore as mediator between the acting self and the acted-upon world. This brings to light the practical finitude. For, the other side of power is impotence. The habit facilitating the use of power actually constricts, so that, in affecting myself by the acquisition of a new habit, there arises a kind of human nature, so that spontaneous beginning is lessened. (HF, 73) Thus, habit narrows. "Habit fixes our tastes, our aptitudes and so restricts our field of availability; . . . my life has taken shape." (HF, 74) Ricœur sees this as a tendency of life to imitate the thing. Practical finitude is the form of perseverance of freedom's tendency to persevere in the act which constitutes being. (HF, 74)

Ricœur points out that a return could be made to the same themes, starting from an analysis of time to show the same dialectic of innovation and sedimentation. "In this way finitude is first perspective, then self-delection, and then inertia or form of perseverance." (HF, 75) Thus we see what constitutes the affective and practical perspective of my existence.

This analysis has revealed the extension of finitude to the aspects of human reality which had become problematical on the transcendental level. Ricœur brings these together in the idea of character, which adds to them the idea of totality, "the finite totality of my existence. Character is the finite openness of my existence taken as a whole." (HF, 75) Character, then, expresses the total closing of the fundamental openness of my own particular closed openness.

"Perspective is my finitude for the thing," (HF, 76) while character is my finitude in all respects, the totality of my finitude. From the depth of feeling there is the power of total expression so that the totality of character can be found in a single expression of feeling if we choose well the one feeling (HF, 77) as an expressive act. Character thus is revealed as a perspectival orientation, as the "limited openness of our field of motivation taken as a whole." (HF, 77) Thus, character is my accessibility to all that is human. It is my humanity "seen from somewhere." (HF, 77) "My humanity is this fundamental accessibility to all that is human outside myself; that community makes every man my like." (HF, 77-78) And character is unalterable, in the sense that no movement can change this zero origin of my total field of motivation – "this non-chosen origin of all my choices." (HF, 79) Character is indistinguishable from the fact of my existence.

Birth designates that my existence is a fate. It also designates heredity, my existence as received from another. Thus, taking the guideline from the transcendental level of reflection as openness and its perspectival origin, Ricœur has shown perspective enriched with affective and practical aspects which are expressed in the notion of totality – character, "immutable and inherited nature." (HF, 80) "Then the destiny of character and of heredity reveals its meaning: it is the given, factual narrowness of my free openness to the ensemble of the possibilities of being-man." (HF, 81)

Happiness

Reflection on desirability reveals the bipolarity of desire: anchored in affection of self, and its openness onto an infinite horizon – happiness, beatitude.[9] ". . . Happiness designates the presence to human activity considered as a totality of the end which will fulfill it." This would be the fulfillment and achievement of the total field of motivation. Thus it is clear why Ricœur wants to think character and happiness as "a constitutive antinomy of human reality. Character is the perspectival orientation of the total field of motivation; happiness is the end toward which all my motivation is orientated. Zero point and horizon." [10]

Following his transcendental guideline, Ricœur sees the necessity of relating happiness to meaning. He is looking for the totality of meaning of the properly human act (HF, 82) "of man's existential project considered as an indivisible whole." (HF, 83) Happiness then is a whole and not merely a sum and therefore must be connected to reason, the demand in man for totality. For Kant, this demand for totality looses itself in illusion – the illusion of reason, and involves the view into the "other" order, the noumenal.

This for Ricœur is the idea of totality, not restricted to the theoretical, but extended also to the will. Thus it is the source of the extreme human disproportion: in human action, the tension between the finitude of character and the infinitude of happiness; (HF, 84-85) character as origin and happiness as infinite end.

Respect

The synthesis between character and happiness in the practical realm is a synthesis in the person *as the self*. However, just as in the theoretical order, the practical synthesis is still a projected synthesis: "The self is aimed at rather than lived." (HF, 86) This self-consciousness is only the consciousness of the self in the representation of the ideal of the self or the person. Ricœur calls this project which I represent to myself as the ideal of a

[9] Paul Ricœur, "The Antinomy of Human Reality," p. 398.
[10] *Ibid.,* p. 398.

person's humanity. Thus "humanity is the person's personality, just as objectivity was the thing's thingness," (HF, 87) and just as the objectivity was the mode of being of the thing, humanity is the mode of being of a human being on which empirical appearance should be patterned. It is the ontological constitution of the human being.

Just as it was on the thing that reflection moved to perspective, meaning (or verb and expression) and synthesis, so now it is on the idea of the person that it progresses to synthesis in this practical order. (HF, 87-88) In thinking "man" or the person a new kind of synthesis is aimed at, that of the Kantian end, placing a symmetry between the synthesis of the thing and the synthesis of the person that is not actually explicit in Kant. The key is that this synthesis is practical and that it is intentional. The self in self-consciousness, distinguished from consciousness in general of the theoretical order, is an end to be achieved in existence. Ricœur has put the self of self-consciousness in the practical consciousness, and therefore, as something to *be done*, a task, a practical intention. Thus this self is a projected self.

The specific experience in which this synthesis is constituted is the moral feeling that Kant called respect. This is an extension of the transcendental imagination, and differs from the use of Kant. This respect has to be in incentive. It has to enable pure practical reason, which Kant has first established, to be necessarily law-giving to the desire in order to be a source of movement to action. As an incentive in the Kantian sense, it becomes the subjective determining ground of the will undetermined by necessity. On the one hand, reason influences the faculty of desire, and on the other hand, the sensibility becomes accessible to reason. (HF, 91) An a priori feeling produced by reason is necessary.

This elevation of desire to reason is the birth of self-esteem. It is here in this practical synthesis that Ricœur again finds man's fragility. The existential fault causing man's fragility arises from the twofold belonging to two worlds, in Kantian language, to the noumenal and the phenomenal . . . "so that the person as belonging to the world of sense is subject to his own personality so far as he belongs to the intelligible world." [11] (91-92)

Ricœur takes great pains to draw out where Kant is wrought with ethical prejudice. He cannot agree with the Kantian presupposition of an already fallen sensibility, but, following the guidelines of his transcendental beginnings, he wishes in this practical order to take the primal, just as he does in the strictly theoretical investigation. This is perhaps the strongest reason for his following the transcendental guidance from the beginning,

[11] Immanuel Kant, *Critique de la raison pratique,* p. 15.

that in the theoretical, the sensibility is not taken as fallen but as primal. He, however, uses the same passions in his own later elucidation as Kant, the passions of greed, power, and glory, but he uses them to come to this primal structure underlying the perverted and "before" the perversion. He therefore wishes to get beneath the sensibility disfigured by these "passions" and away from the dualism which this view of the passions entails, as has been indicated in the second chapter of this study. Ricœur's objection to sensibility as fallen instead of primal is levied against an ethical vision of the world more than against that of Kant. (HF, 92) It is fundamental to Ricœurean philosophy that access can be had from the fallen to that *from which* the fall comes.

Pure Reflection on the Affective

After introducing respect as an a priori moral feeling as produced by reason on sensibility, Ricœur takes up a fuller discussion of feeling in relation to fallibility in disproportion, especially disproportion of feeling as affective fragility. His hope is to some extent to close the gap between the previous reflection and the *pathétique* of misery as the pre-philosophical beginning of this whole reflection.

This would be the third level of the disproportion of man. The first moment of fragility was the transcendental imagination of theoretical consciousness or consciousness in general. It transcends itself intentionally in its correlate, the thing. The second moment of fragility, that of self-consciousness, was respect, which was transcended in the presentation of the self or the person, still an "objectival" synthesis. (HF, 98) This third moment, the restless heart, the *thumos* of Plato, that of the affective, of feeling, would be the fragile moment *par excellence*. It becomes clear that this is due to the interiorization of feeling, bringing the disproportion inside.

However this level of the discussion of disproportion in feeling brings up the methodological problem of a philosophy of feeling brought to the level of reason, in the sense of reason as a demand not simply for the pure and the radical, but rather for the total, the concrete. (HF, 98) This is still an attempt to fill the gap between the purely transcendental reflection of disproportion and the lived experience of misery put forth in the *pathétique*. (HF, 98) But it must remain philosophical, and not become *pathétique*. Ricœur sees this as possible because . . . "if then, this pathos was already mythos, that is, speech, it must be possible to restore it in the dimension of philosophic discourse." (HF, 99) This is a serious statement, that if it is already in the sphere of speech, it is not devoid of all thematic structure, and can be raised from its proper language to philosophical discourse. This is the attempt of this chapter of Ricœur's *L'homme faillible,* which now must be analysed with a view to its "language proper to it," of myth and rhetoric, especially with regard to the return to myth and symbols as the language of experience, specifically of the experience of evil.

Twofold Direction of Feeling

Ricœur will attempt to gain insight into feeling by seeing its function as inverse to that of knowledge. Whereas knowledge, in objectivating, puts objects as such at a distance and separates them from the knower, feeling interiorizes, bringing inside. (HF, 99) However, he is careful not to end up in emotionalism or affectivism, pointing out that he considers the two, feeling and knowledge, both to be primordial and not giving any priority to feeling. (HF, 99) Since he sees that the significance of feeling appears in "the reciprocal genesis of knowing and feeling," (HF, 99) he approaches feeling together with knowing in an intentional analysis.

This intentional analysis will establish them in their reciprocity. It also brings out and is centered on the unity of the intentional and the affective tendencies of feelings. This development by Ricœur is crucial to his whole thinking, as preliminary to the theory of linguistic expressions. It is from his theory of feeling that we must take our point of departure and foundation for discussing his symbolic function or linguistic expressions with a double meaning, which express and hide at the same time, and which demand deciphering to get to their real meaning.

Ricœur is especially trying to bring out three points in this intentional analysis of feeling: first, the unity of intentionality and affection in feeling; and secondly, the connection between the objectivity of knowing and this intentionality of feeling; and thirdly, that only insofar as it is intentional does feeling manifest its affection, so that to cut off intentionality of feeling is to cut off its revealing power as ability to reveal the interior.

The unity of intentionality and affection in feeling

Beginning this intentional analysis of feeling to bring out the relation between, for example, love and the lovable, hate and the hateful, on an horizontal level, Ricœur finds this relation as that set up by feeling between the self and the world to be a paradox or an *"aporia."* (HF, 100) The uniqueness of this intentionality of feeling is that while it designates qualities felt-feeling of something – it also reveals the way the self is inwardly affected. (HF, 100-101) Also, even though their intentionality is not to be denied, the correlates of feelings cannot be called objects since they must be founded in the objects already there. "It is the perceived and known object which endows them with a center of significance, a pole of objectivity . . ." (HF, 127-128) Thus it is the percept of the observed thing or present person which gives exteriority and which is needed in order to bring these "correlates" of the hateful or the lovable to the light of the world. (HF, 127-128) Feeling does not posit any being in what it aims at. (HF, 101) Feeling rather manifests the affection of the soul on the thing already posited as there. Thus feeling manifests our relation to the world which relation is pre-reflective or pre-objective. (HF, 101) It reveals our complicity with and our belonging to the world. "But because we live in the subject-object duality which has educated our language, this relation can only be reached indirectly." (HF, 101)

Ricœur points out the unity between the tendency "of behavioristic psychology and this intentionality of feeling, in order to deepen the grasp of the reciprocity between knowing and feeling. He considers the "objective direction" of the behaviorists as the same as his "aim" of feeling. But the behaviorist must realize that his use of "energy," "drive," "equilibrium" is a metaphorical language, and it is the intentional analysis that restores the meaning. Feeling is not part of a whole, but a significant moment of the whole. (HF, 102-103)

Ricœur considers the other challenger of the privileged position as revealer of connections with the beings of the world to be that of depth psychology. He does not disagree with them that there must be a suspicion of the apparent sense and a consequent movement by hermeneutics to a more real latent sense. He simply points out that it is this apparent sense which manifest the drives into the dimension of signifying even though it may dissimilate them.

Feeling must be understood by the contrast between the detaching over against us and objectifying of things and beings, and the movement by which we somehow appropriate and interiorize them. (HF, 105) Ricœur also sees the unity of intentionality and affection of feeling as the sign of the mystery of feeling which is the paradoxical "indivisible connection of my existence with beings and being through desire and love." (HF, 105) Also, feeling can be described only paradoxically because of the objectivity in which our language has been worked out. Since our language is such, we must be careful in speaking of feeling.

Since feeling is contemporaneous with knowledge, interiorizing what knowledge objectifies, and since feeling manifests what life aims at, it becomes clear that the disproportion of knowing is reflected and completed in the disproportion of feeling. This is the point to which Ricœur has been moving, the disproportion of feeling and its affective fragility. Following what he calls the first benefit of the mutual genesis of knowing and feeling, he moves from merely horizontal analysis of feeling to a vertical analysis of the degrees of feeling according to the degrees of objects. (HF, 107) Thus the intermediate term will move into the life of feeling, and move to the interior of man instead of on the object or on the idea of man. This disproportion is in the inner conflict of desire, the *thumos*.

Affective disproportion

Continuing to follow his initial transcendental reflection presenting perspective and meaning as guideline, Ricœur begins with the primordial disproportion between vital desire and intellectual desire or love, i.e., with *epithumia* and *eros*. "Man's humanity is that fluctuation in levels, that initial polarity, that divergence of affective tension between the extremities of which the 'heart' is placed." (HF, 109) This is Ricœur's working hypothesis. He establishes this hypothesis by showing that there are two kinds of terminations of affective movements: pleasure, which fulfills or culminates or perfects particular acts or processes; and happiness, now the fullness of happiness; and not the abstract or empty happiness opposed to character, but a happiness which is the perfection of the total work of man, the termination of his existential project as a whole. It is the inner discord of these two terminations which internally divides human desire. (HF, 109)

Ricœur's analysis of pleasure and the conflict of desire as affective disproportion precedes pleasure as evil or as fallen. Rather, his is an analysis of pleasure as perfection before it is tarnished with the view of it which puts it in the negative vein of evil.

The main point in this development is precisely the same as in his transcendental analysis of knowing: that happiness eclipses pleasure, that we grasp the limitation, the finitude of pleasure by grasping the transgression of it in happiness.

Pleasure is perfection, but a finite one, and finite for two reasons; first, it is the perfection, the fulfillment only of *particular acts,* and only of the instant; and secondly, because it is the perfection of the *bodily life,* bringing out my organic rootedness in the world. (HF, 110) This rootedness shows the priority of living as the existential condition of all other activities. Nevertheless, pleasure is total just as happiness, but it is total only in the instant. This is an important point for Ricœur because . . . "it is precisely this compression of happiness into the instant which threatens to arrest the dynamism of acting in the celebration of *Living*." (Ricœur's italics) Thus

Ricœur sees in this the threat of a closing off of the horizon of happiness in the finite, but *only* the threat. (HF, 111) That is why he can disagree with those who begin with pleasure as already in the downfall and as already evil. He accuses them of confusing pleasure's attachment to living with an already actual and prior fall. (HF, 111) To cut myself off from the higher horizon is a blindness with a hindrance springing from it. I am responsible for both.

This finitude of pleasure has as its beyond a happiness which would then be the perfect pleasure. Pleasure can both arrest us on the level of living, or can merge with happiness, and yield perfect pleasure. Ricœur finds a certain suspension of pleasure necessary, however, to come to happiness as its perfect form, following Aristotle here in going back to the principle of activity and its excellence or virtue. Thus the idea of happiness in the dialectic of character and happiness as a demand for totality is enriched by affective meaning and thus receives its affective plenitude. (HF, 114-115)

Ricœur wishes to renew this dialectic of pleasure and happiness of the ancient Greek thinking in terms of the contemporary psychology of vital feelings and the philosophy (ontology) of spiritual feeling. This dialectic will take us to the fullness of the unity of intention and affection in feeling. (HF, 119)

In reworking this ancient dialectic between pleasure and happiness, Ricœur begins with the contemporary psychology of vital feelings, bringing out its inadequacies first from within. He does this by beginning with their role of feeling as regulative and functional. Feeling in this context is the recovery of equilibrium. (HF, 115) He wishes to question the most general presupposition of this normativity, "the idea of adaptation to a supposedly given environment." (HF, 115) What Ricœur wishes to question is the extension of an adaptive scheme valid in animal psychology to anthropology. (HF, 115-116) He does not wish to deny the validity of this extention. Rather, it is necessary to see that the situation which the concepts of adaptability describe is indeed a human situation, but one reduced and simplified, oblivious to the ontological destination of human desire, and mimicking "the vital in the cultural." Since in the strict sense the criterion of adaptation holds only for vital feeling and only in a limited way, this criterion must be extended, as is quite clear in many human situations. Ricœur moves from tasks to the level of pretension with regard to social roles. (HF, 116)

The movement has been from the idea of task defined by norms to the idea of a level of pretensions. This latter is determined by both society and the personality. This introduction of such inexactness, indefiniteness, renders unusable the ideas of equilibrium. (HF, 117) But since most often we treat ourselves as objects, we tend to render valid these concepts at least to some extent. "But this objectified existence" (HF, 111) is not exhaustive of the fundamental possibilities of man. Here Ricœur wishes to criticize this tendency to identify feeling with affective regulation by bringing in the other pole, spiritual feeling and philosophy of feeling as ontological. Thus he will bring in another mode of ontological feeling rather than that giving rise to objectified (scientific) existence.

In this consideration, Ricœur will instate reason in the Kantian sense as a demand for totality in its place in the affective field. The psychology of feeling is blind without the philosophy or reason. (HF, 118) Within the realm of the affective, in affective confusion, reason is what distinguishes the pleasure intention from the happiness intention. Thus Ricœur wants to uncover the reason, the demand for totality, the infinite in the affective, in feeling. This moment Ricœur refers to as "an affective openness in the closing of Care." (HF, 118)

In unifying reason and feeling Ricœur indicates two points in their reciprocity which are most important and fundamental to this whole development of his theory of feeling. 1. For him, it is reason as an openness to totality which constitutes or engenders feeling as an openness to happiness. 2. But it is feeling which interiorizes reason, showing me that it is my reason, that "feeling ... is the very belonging of existence to the being whose reason is thinking." (HF, 119) This is the full expression of the identity of intention and affection in feeling. Feeling attests that being is not entirely other, that whatever it is, it is the primordial space in which we continue to exist. (HF, 119)

The schematization of this fundamental feeling and its particularization is in a diversity of feelings of belonging. This schematization is in the direction of the "we" and of "Ideas" or tasks of supra-personal works. The infinitude of feeling becomes evident from the lack of completion, the failure to exhaust the demand for totalization in the particular culture, politic, or economy.

Ricœur proceeds to evolve several conclusions or consequences from this brief schematization of ontological feeling. *First,* by means of it, he arrives at the polarity of what he calls Care and Heart. He opposes the openness and availability of Heart to the greed of the body and living. For him, sacrifice is the form which takes on the heart's transcendence, showing the fundamental unity of the two schemata of belonging, that of friendship, and that of devotion. (HF, 120) "Friendship is to another what devotion is to the idea, and the two together constitute perspective-*Aussicht* – 'on an order in which, alone, we can continue to exist.' " (HF, 120)

The *second* consequence Ricœur draws from this schematization of ontological feeling is that it helps to solve some of the difficulties with regard to ontological feeling. It is of extreme importance that here Ricœur speaks of feeling as a promise, an anticipation, more than as a possession, so that spiritual feelings are feelings of the transition toward happiness. Happiness is designated by its signs, and these signs of happiness are accessible only from the point of view of a character. And since there are many ways to be oriented to fulfillment, to happiness, a topology of happiness is possible. (HF, 120)

Third, the idea of the schematization of feeling allows for the accounting of feelings with an ontological bearing, those which are essentially formless or atmospheric feelings or moods. (HF, 121) ". . . Through their formless character they designate the fundamental feeling of which the determined feelings are the schemata, namely, *the very openness of man to being.*" (HF, 121) As a consequence of the general intentional structure of feeling, all feelings can acquire form or can return to a formless state. They take on form by fastening onto the objects of knowledge, and return to the formless by going back into life, in interiorization, in introspection. For Ricœur there is a feeling of the unconditioned which is formless. Moods, in interiorizing, bring into the "heart of our heart" the absolute, as the unconditioned, which is demanded by reason and which feeling manifests as interior. (HF, 122)

Fourth, he considers the positive and negative ontological feeling as two sides of the same ontological feeling. For him, "Joy . . . is the only affective mood worthy of being called ontological. Anguish is only its underside or absence and distance." (HF, 122) Thus he has arrived at affective fragility, that man is capable of joy in and through anguish. This is the radical principle of all disproportion in feeling, indicating the true significance of conflict.

Ricœur wishes to stabilize his working hypothesis under the guidance of the polarity between the finite and infinite, between the resolution of pleasure and of happiness. Through a study of the dynamics of affectivity he wishes to come from the synthesis on the object to a median, a third term as synthesis, but this time interiorized with the feelings and therefore accessible to the heart or to the heart's humanity. (HF, 123) He places this median of the affective life under Plato's *thumos* as the region situated between the vital and the spiritual affections, or "all the affectivity which makes up the transition between living and thinking . . ." (HF, 123) Also, it is in this region of the *thumos* that the self is constituted, as desire taking on the characteristics of otherness and subjectivity constitutive of a self. And on the other hand, the self spills over in feelings of belonging to "we," to a community and to an idea. Thus the self is revealed as intermediary, as between two, as a transition. (HF, 123) He attempts to avoid several difficulties or objections against past theories of passions and of feeling and to arrive at this difference of the self from other selves and from things prior to its corruption underneath the passions as expressed in corruption, to their primordial state, to "the innocence of 'difference.' " (HF, 124)

Ricœur at the outset follows Kant in beginning with interhuman, cultural, and social passions. Traditional treatments of passions and of appetites have failed to treat the intersubjective adequately and have missed the introduction of a new realm with that of the person. The arduous of the irascible appetites and the love of benevolence hint or lead to it, but they are both reduced to the thing, to the good or the bad object, and do not introduce this new objectivity. Yet for him, the "encountering of another person is what breaks the finite, cyclic pattern of the sensible appetite. (HF, 127)

However, he sees the necessity of avoiding Kant's prejudice. Kant does not put himself before specifically human passions, but as fallen forms of human affectivity which may have been all right for him in his pragmatic anthropology, but is not adequate for a fundamental anthropology. Ricœur insists on the possibility of beginning with these same passions as Kant, but wishes to go on to their primordial state which is revealed in and through these corrupt expressions. He wishes to discover the authentic *Suchen* behind Kant's triple *Sucht,* the quest of humanity constitutive of *praxis* and self, and not the fallen and mad quest. To arrive thus at the primordial state under Kant's quests, Ricœur points out that, although we know these fundamental quests *empirically* as fallen, we understand these passions in their essence only as a perversion of . . . i.e., to grasp these as fallen presupposes this primordial state, which is grasped in imagination of the state of innocence. This is the imaginative variation of Husserl, which is so important to Ricœurian philosophy. He hopes to arrive at the essence through the fact or by breaking away from the fact to the possibility and so to the essence. (HF, 128) The passions understood as bad or fallen require the understanding of the passions as innocent in another empirical manifestation or modality, in the primordial state grasped by the imagination. (HF, 128)

In this investigation, Ricœur proposes to follow objectivity as guide. He follows that objectivity which is correlative to the feelings of having, power, and worth. This is not the objectivity of the thing, of the natural object, but rather that of the extension of objectivity to the cultural order. He wants also to extend the intersubjectivity of the world from an abstract mutuality of seeing to the economic, political, and cultural dimensions of objectivity making a human world. He wants to show the new aspects of objectivity interiorized in these feelings as objectivity not set over against myself as object. (HF, 128-129) What is more important than this new relation to things is the new relations these human quests establish with other persons. It is in this sphere of discussion that the constitution of the self comes to light, and not in the intersubjectivity of seeing. Thus this consideration of having, power and worth is one of great importance to Ricœur, since in or under these quests we can discover primordial states which constitute the self. (HF, 129)

By means of the objectivity which is built on these themes of having, power, and worth, Ricœur wishes to spell out the relationship of the self to another self. (HF, 129) It is necessary to some extent at least to follow the main lines and moments of his development in this most important phase of unfolding the meaning of human reality.

The new dimension of the object serving as guide is the economic which can also serve to distinguish human need from animal need. This economic object is not simply an object as good or bad or the arduous of such, but is the *available* good. What Ricœur proposes to do at this stage is to unfold the innocent having from the fallen. Although appropriation is the source in history of some of the greatest alienations, it still presupposes the appropriation which is constituting of the "I" constituted by being founded on the "mine." (HF, 130)

It is work which distinguishes the animal environment and the human world, and which establishes this new relation to things, the *economic relation*, ". . . whereas the animal merely preserves itself, man subsists and establishes himself among things in treating them as possessions." (HF, 130)

Ricœur has so far been focusing on the objectivity which he has taken as guide. Now he moves further back from the object to the originality of the feelings attached to having. It is the *availability for me* of the thing which brings about the feelings relative to acquisition and appropriation, to possession and preservation. (HF, 130) Since now he is trying to reach the affection of the I in the feelings as feeling, he points out that what is properly feeling in this case is "the interiorization of the relation to the economic thing, the resonance of the having in the "I" under the form of the 'mine.' " (HF, 130) There are two sides of this feeling of having; first, the control over the having, and second, the dependence on something other than myself. The threat of loosing what is mine constitutes the otherness of the mine, bringing out the distance between the "I" and the mine. Thus what is mine is mine only as long as I hold onto it. (HF, 130)

This interiorization of feeling also brings out the different manners of relation to another – the mine and the yours. What is mine is not yours, and what is yours is not mine. Ricœur considers this exclusion of differentiation begun by the body which is a separate and different spatiality, to extend from the body to what is the body's, i.e., a house for the body, etc. . . . and spreading from the body to the mind, as my ideas. Yet he explicity protects the ego from total differentiation, pointing out that each ego "retains a ring of spiritual indifferentiation" (HF, 131) in order to preserve the commonness necessary for communication, and to make the other not only different but my like. Imaginative variation indicates the essence of having in innocence. There cannot be man without having, there cannot be I without the mine, even in denying the private appropriation of the "I." The "We" and "Our" mediate the "I" and the "Mine." It is the primordial state, the innocent having, which is presupposed by the bad having so that the *Habsucht* of Kant is a perversion of it. (HF, 132)

From the economic relations of having Ricœur turns to the relation of power to look for an innocent quest underlying the perversion of domination. The relations of having themselves introduce the relations of power. Again Ricœur begins with the objectivity and then moves from this as guide to the interior feelings.

There are two relations of power of man over man implied in the relation of man to having, (HF, 132); the economic-social, and the technological. Ricœur proceeds to unfold these two ways power is implied in having, proceeding from one stage to the next by analysis.

He begins with a consideration of work as dealing with the forces of nature in relation to the forces of work involved in the power of man over man. The forces of work are similar to those of nature, to be conquered or organized for efficient production. However, the subordination in work of operations is not that of persons. This subordination in work becomes a relation of command and obedience only in the structures, the form, defined by the economic and social system and the institutional body, and not only the technology of work. The task itself is the source of such levels of human work. (HF, 133) Thus it is clear that having leads to power, since the one or group who possesses or manages is the one who has power over the works. Even in the event that the two are the same, the distinction between the relations of subordination, that of the technological and that of the social, are not destroyed. (HF, 133-134)

Political power is introduced as that authority which sanctions the institutions which allow for the other relations of domination or other forms of power. Thus the political power is seen as the more dominant power which guarantees the means of production by fostering the institutions with its authority. (HF, 134) But this political sphere, related to the passions through this power, must not be reduced simply and totally to passion. For Ricœur, authority or power is not bad in itself; rather, such an interpretation of it presupposes the good power or authority in terms of which it is bad. This is manifested or arrived at through imaginative variation, which yields the essence of having. "The command is a necessary 'differentiation' among men and is implied in the essence of the political sphere" (HF, 134). It comes out in that it is power of man or men over other men in an institution.

This power of man over other men in an institution is the new object Ricœur takes up to lead inside to the interior as guide into a world of feelings which relates to this human power. It is this object as the form in which the "interhuman relation of power is realized" which is the order principle of these feelings. (HF, 135)

Ricœur brings out further justification by simple exposition and analysis of his procedure of the reciprocity of knowing and feeling which was analyzed before. He again is able to connect this "objectivity" of power with the affectivity of feeling. Affectivity of feeling as a passive modification of the self attaches itself to objects of a high order to become human. (HF, 135) Not only is Ricœur involving and employing the reciprocity of knowing and feeling, but also what he has explained as the unity of the intentionality and the affectivity of feeling. Starting with the object and engaging in a somewhat intentional analysis, he has effectively uncovered the affection peculiar to feelings of power, of power over, and of being under power. But this does not yet go far enough for him. He still must achieve the essential, he must distinguish the feelings relating to power from passion of power, in that power is not necessarily and always fallen. Reflecting on power as an established reality, as object, Ricœur sees good cause to consider power as essentially tied up with evil, first because it corrupts passion only by violence as violent power, and second, because as such it is always already fallen. This still presupposes the innocent power in terms of which I can see power as fallen, as evil, and as perversion. This is the imagining of power without violence, which would be an authority or non-violent power to educate to freedom, one which does not contradict freedom. Ricœur considers this essence of power yielded by imagination as first, governing "all efforts to transform power into an education to freedom"; and second, discovering power as primordially inherent in man. (HF, 136)

The feelings which are at the root of the passions of power are the source of the passions which derange them. And it is these pure feelings which ground man as a political animal. (HF, 136)

Ricœur now looks for the basic quest behind the third of Kant's passions in his anthropology, that of honor or the quest for worth in the eyes of another. (HF, 136-137) Again he will try to arrive at the *constituting feeling* from the deranged passion, through imaginative variation arriving at the essence.

This interhuman relation of a quest for esteem of others adds to the other two interhuman relations already gone through the aspect of reciprocity, or demand for reciprocity not in the others which were not reciprocal relations. Thus it is in this realm of the interpersonal that the self reaches or seeks to reach its constitution beyond that of the economic and political spheres. This constitution of the self is dependent on the esteem, approval and recognition of others, so that my existence for myself depends on another's opinion. (HF, 137) To some extent, at least, the self is dependent and is received from the opinion of the other.

The self's existence is fragile because the esteem establishing it is merely opinion, *doxa,* belief: *time is doxa.* This realm of opinion, or recognition as basic to esteem is what keeps this quest within the median zone of affectivity between the vital and the spiritual. (HF, 137-138) Since it is in the realm of *thumos* and not creative, it is not in the realm of *eros,* yet it is aligned with *eros,* which is schematized and finds in esteem a good ally. (HF, 138)

Having already been guided by the objectivity first of the economic good in the quest for having and by the objectivity of political institutions of the quest for power, Ricœur looks to the objectivity of the quest for esteem in *existence-worth,* which is for him what Kant calls ends in themselves, and not simply ends to be realized. Thus they do not become a value, or have a worth for me because of my action, but rather, persons for Kant are ends in themselves. Kant calls this objectivity humanity, the idea of man in me or in another, as we have seen when Ricœur treated the practical disproportion. For Ricœur it is the other person's esteem which conveys my humanity to me and makes it known to me. However, this objectivity of the idea of humanity as formal is expressed in the material objectivity of cultural works which express this humanity. (HF, 139) " 'Works' of art and literature, and, in general, works of the mind, insofar as they mirror not merely an environment and an epoch but search out man's possibilities, are the real 'objects' which manifest the abstract universality of the idea of humanity through their concrete universality." (HF, 139) Thus Ricœur has traced the forward movement of objectivity from having, to power, to worth, arriving at the last of these in cultural objectivity, the relation of man to man, which is represented in the idea of humanity as its abstract form. "It is this formal and material objectivity of the idea of man which engenders an affectivity to its measure: the cycle of the feelings of esteem." (HF, 140)

Self-esteem is then the same kind of esteem I have for others, "If humanity is what I esteem in another and in myself, I esteem myself as though for another." (HF, 140) Self-esteem is then, an indirect relation which is mediated through the esteem of another from myself to myself only through the esteem of the other. This highest point to which self-consciousness is raised by being constituted by the feeling of my worth is based on opinion or belief and is not knowledge. It is only *doxa* in that I believe I am worth something from the opinion of another, and mine is only an experience of opinion. (HF, 140)

1. This basis of self-esteem on belief or opinion is what makes it possible to err. For, as opinion, it can be wrong, mistaken, sham; or it can be vain or neglected and offset by self-overestimation, by a turning against the esteem of others because of neglect of my own, etc. . . . but all of which demand the quest for recognition to be understood. (HF, 141) Thus it becomes evident how the self and the other are constituted in the content of belief, the *noema* of the feeling of worth. (HF, 141) To understand ourselves or others we turn to this genesis of affective meaning.

2. This basis of esteem, of self-esteem, on belief or opinion also gives rise to the possibility of a pathology of esteem. But Ricœur always insists on the understanding of the pathological form of self-esteem from the non-pathological form or the non-fallen form.

3. This basis of esteem and self-esteem on belief or opinion also is the possibility of the moral perversions of this feeling. Because of this aspect of feeling, its corruption is possible. However, between this possibility of corruption and its actuality and actual experience there is a great distance for Ricœur since the actual condition is not necessarily one of corruption even though *de facto* it might be. Ricœur puts it this way: "Between self-esteem and vain-glory there is the whole distance which separates the possibility of evil and its advent; (HF, 141)." But it is still the primordial feeling that makes pathology possible and not vice versa. The blindness

necessary for vanity of perversion is not constituting, not essential, but comes, is accepted. (HF, 141) It is this vanity which prevents the belief which transforms the quest for recognition into the passion for honor. (HF, 141)

Affective Fragility

Ricœur feels he has arrived at the deepest level of disproportion of man in that of feeling, the disproportion which he calls affective fragility, or the disproportion between vital feeling and spiritual feeling. He has already turned to pleasure and happiness as that which terminates the vital desire and the intellectual desire. Now he wishes to turn to the completion or termination of the thymic quests, of having, of power, and of worth, to see how their consummation brings out the duality of pleasure and happiness or the finite and the infinite of feeling. (HF, 142) He wishes to reveal the instability, the precariousness of the *thumos* in two steps; first, as situation between the two, the vital and the spiritual; and second, as their mixture.

1. The mode of the fulfillment of the *thumos* reveals its position as unstable, since the fulfillment is not complete, and the self is never certain. This introduces a note of indefiniteness with its endless pursuit. Thus human action unfolding from these "three fundamental quests of self-being" is a perpetual movement. (HF, 142) All action is open instead of terminal. Ricœur likes to call this undetermined terminus, after Hegel, desire of desire. Since pleasure or pain can thus become contributors for further activity, so that . . ." human action regenerates and nourishes itself of itself, drawn forward by its insatiable quests." (HF, 143)

2. The *thumos* must be seen for Ricœur as the mixture of the vital and the spiritual, instead of simply situated between them. (HF, 144) Affective fragility then is expressed in the relation of these indefinite or incomplete quests as it relates to, mixes with, and exchanges with, the vital level and with the spiritual desire for happiness. (HF, 144)

The triple quests make the vital human. Ricœur takes as an example par excellence sexuality, which in man is not simple instinct, but is made human by these quests, with the quest of reciprocity as the culmination and most humanizing aspect. Sexual satisfaction is no longer simply physical satisfaction. (HF, 144)

Quests and the Spiritual

The *thumos* undergoes the attraction of the spiritual as well as that of the vital. It is in this new mixture that Ricœur sees the affective drive of great passions. (HF, 145) The transcending movement of the "great" passions is not accounted for by passion-affection nor passion-unreason. It must be connected to the desire for happiness and not to the desire to live. (HF, 146) In fact, it is this view which determines how he defines passion. Instead of taking it as encompassing all feelings as passive, as the tradition tended to do, he calls passion only "that class of feelings which cannot be accounted for by a derivation from the vital feelings" or within the horizon of pleasure. (HF, 145) This transcending intention which dwells in passion of such force can only be accounted for by its connection to the infinite attraction of happiness, as flowing from it. Thus, "man puts all his strength and his whole heart into passion because a subject of desire has become all for him." (HF, 146) But Ricœur does not wish to leave it in this level of the vague. He sees in passion the mixture of the unlimited desire of the *thumos* and the desire for happiness. The impassioned person has put his "all" in one of the objects which have been seen as the correlates of having, of power, or of worth (of possession, of domination, or of valoration.) Thus one of these objects represents the all of the desirable. "One might say that the infinitude of happiness descends to the indefinite of restlessness." (HF, 146) The desire of desire of *thumos* offers its objects in representations and images to the objectless aim of happiness. This for Ricœur is the source and occasion of illusion and mistake. But there is something more primordial than this underlying mistake and illusion, which he calls the affective figuration of happiness in the *thumos*.

Thus passion receives its force and abandon from *Eros,* and its restlessness from *thumos,* both of which are presupposed by the false infinite of passion. Ricœur here indicates what he sees from the spiritual desire in passion underlying all passions as their possibility. The impassioned man puts his whole desire for happiness in one of these objects in which the self is constituted. This for Ricœur is the schematization of happiness in the themes of *thumos.* (HF, 147) Thus we reach the climactic point of Ricœur's development and must see this as he says it:

... Only a being who wants the all and who schematizes it in the objects of human desire is able to make a mistake, that is, take his object for the *absolute, forget* the symbolic character of the bond between happiness and an object of desire; this forgetting makes the symbol an idol; the impassioned life becomes a passional existence. This forgetting, this birth of the idol, of servitude and passional sufferance, leads to a hermeneutics of the passions which we will undertake elsewhere. But it was necessary to show the point of impact of the passions in a primordial affection which is the very locus of fallibility. The restless devotedness of the impassioned is like the primordial innocence of the passional, and at the same time the essential fragility from where it originated.

Nowhere better than in the relation of the impassioned to the passional do we understand that the structures of fallibility make up the pre-existing ground of fault. (HF, 147)

Thus we have followed Ricœur to the depth of human disproportion in feeling. It is the function of feeling first to bind to things, to beings, to Being. This has been revealed by the unity of its intentionality and affection brought to light in the reciprocity with knowing and objectivity.

But it also brought to light the inner conflict of the self with the self which is presupposed for bringing inside the exterior conflicts in culture and in history.

CHAPTER IV

EIDETICS, EXISTENCE, AND EXPERIENCE

INTRODUCTION

This chapter is meant to make the transition from one focus to another somewhat different one. So far, after the first chapter which simply states the basic level of enquiry and the problems aimed at in this work, we have attempted to dwell for the most part on the different modes of pure reflection which Ricœur employs in the first levels of his philosophy of the will. This chapter will conclude that level and attempt to lay the foundation for and make the transition to the various problems which he feels he must confront on a different front in his attempt to work through his hermeneutics of symbols. We shall attempt to deal with his different treatments as he confronted them, and the various detours which distracted him from completing the initial project. However, this is not an attempt to render a rigorous history of the development of his thought, since that would not allow us to remain focused on our project of explicitating his developments and extensions, and then returning to the initial project.

The level reached after the reflecting on structures is that of experience. The discussion now concerns Ricœur's method of access to experience of evil expressed in myth or in the language of avowal. However, the transition from the existential to experience must be further elaborated.

At this point it is necessary to repeat an essential point of difficulty in treating the thinking of Ricœur. It is virtually impossible to treat questions of method independently from questions of doctrine. Therefore, it is necessary in an attempt such as this to deal with the evolution and development of the content or doctrine of Ricœur's thinking at the same time as with the problem of the symbolics.

This chapter will attempt to bring together what has gone before in the previous two chapters with what will come in the next chapters. Thus it will become clear that all that has gone before is an important if not necessary preliminary treatment for this study. Such important themes as signification, *Cogito,* self have emerged as fundamentally important structural levels of the philosophy of the will. It will become clear how these themes develop in the new or reoriented focus of the mythics and symbolics. Also the nature of the symbolic structure emerges more clearly.

ADVANTAGES OF EIDETICS

1. Ricœur has made an important distinction at the very outset of his eidetics. He has upheld the view that underlying the variations of the empirical man and contingency, there is an essential nature presupposed both by innocence and fault, one which can be obtained through the eidetic description. Thus at the outset of his philosophy of the will, great care is taken not to put accidental characteristics on this level of the essential structures of man's willing. One such is culpability. He explicitly opposes himself to any tendency to ontologize fault, to make it a part of man's essential condition, and emphatically asserts its empirical relevance or belonging to man in the concrete. Therefore it must, and not merely can, be bracketed. It must be bracketed in order to give rise in the eidetic to the essential and abstract man, and to the essential structures of willing. Since fault is only an accident, and since eidetics deals with essences, in the Husserlian sense, it must be bracketed, and gives rise to another methodological adjustment to reach this level of the accidental aspects.

2. An essential point of all Ricœur's philosophy is his wish to view man from a global vision, a view on the totality. He emphasises that he wishes to begin his reflection on the whole of man, and not simply from the limitations of man, not simply from the point of view of finitude. He denies that the finitude is the essence of man. The essential nature of man includes both the finite and the infinite, a tendency to both. Thus in looking for the *locus* of evil in man as to its existential possibility, he focuses on disproportion of these two, the finite and the infinite, and their existential synthesis.

3. The essential nature of man reveals the basic unity of the two elements, the finite and the infinite, or in the first part of his philosophy, the unity of the voluntary and the involuntary. In the second part, as treated in the third chapter of our study, this took the form of the synthesis of the two elements on the different levels. This unity, however, has revealed itself as precarious and polemical, in that on trying to get closer to it under analysis and synthesis, it seems to fail and to reveal a deeper duality. Having seen the fragility of the synthesis on the affective level, which

brings this unity home to man, the need is felt to trace the contours of the lived experience in the concrete since this is the next level, and the outcome of a descent directed to the concrete. To what extent this is so is still to be seen. However, it is or will be seen to spring from Ricœur's basic tenet that phenomenology today should need both the beginning of Husserl especially concerning his theory of meaning, and the later Husserl, concerning the lived-world or *Lebenswelt*. The basic tenet referred to here is that consciousness constitutes not everything in it, but only after receiving, so that the link to the world is preserved.

4. Ricœur wishes to turn to the symbols and myths as a means of access to the accidental conditions of man's fault, to his guilt, and also to unfold the unity of man revealed in myths. This has become his mode of approach to the empirical. However, to move too quickly to an ontological hermeneutic from the various hermeneutics already practiced is to miss and to level off too much of man; and to make ontological what is only accidental.

These problems should be reflected upon at greater length to conclude this part and to lead into the next part treating experience with the symbolic language in which it comes to light in expressions with double meanings.

THE EXTENSION TO EXISTENCE

We have already seen in Chapter three how Ricœur has had to go beyond the limitations of the transcendental style of reflection because of its abstract nature, its failure to grasp the other fuller aspects of the world and the thing, the person, and their synthesis. Although some of these themes will be touched upon in the next chapter, it is necessary to elaborate some points concerning the extension to existence and the existential turn of transcendental phenomenology as we have seen it worked out in the last chapter. This will more explicitly approach the need to turn to experience, and in doing so, to turn to symbolic expressions, with all the problems of hermeneutics and symbols this introduces, and the detour and consequent extension.

Ricœur points out in several of his writings that Husserlian phenomenology became more and more existential to the degree that the problem of perception took precedence over all other problems.[1] This to some extent, at least, marks a certain change in Husserl's thought, one which can be seen as a different emphasis on the way of defining consciousness.

---

[1] Paul Ricœur, "Existential Phenomenology" and "Methods and Task of a Phenomenology of the Will," in *Husserl; An Analysis of His Phenomenology*. Also "New Developments in Phenomenology in France," pp. 1-30.

In his earlier works, from the *Logical Investigations* to the *Cartesian Meditations,* consciousness is defined by its distance and its absence, which is the power of signifying or of meaning. The intending of signifying can be *empty* and even incapable of fulfillment, as in the case with absurd propositions. In this manner of viewing consciousness, perception is only a privileged mode of fulfillment by intuition. Thus, consciousness is doubly intentional by virtue of being an intuitive fulfilling. In short, in the first works, consciousness it at once speech and perception.[2]

Ricœur interprets the works of the last ten years as describing perception, the very *presence* of consciousness to things, as the *initial basis* and *genetic origin* of all operations of consciousness.

"This is the consciousness which gives, which sees, which effects presences, and it supports and founds the consciousness which signifies, which judges, and which speaks. This shift in accent marks the passage to existential phenomenology. In fact, the sense of the existence of things and that of the subject are revealed simultaneously in perception thus reinterpreted." [3]

Even with this existential turn of transcendental phenomenology, Husserl never really got away from his logistic prejudice. The problem therefore poses itself for Ricœur on the existential level of his phenomenology of the will whether "the doctrine of transcendental idealism has value only within the limits of a theory of representation, of the spectator consciousness." [4] For Husserl this was not so great a problem, because he considered the affective and the volitive subjective process to be founded on representation.[5] This for Ricœur does not stand up to a direct reflection on practical life, as can be seen from his *Le volontaire et l'involontaire,* and from *L'homme faillible.* Such a reflection on practical life will reveal that willing has a way of "giving sense to the world by opening up practical possibilities and penetrating the indeterminate zones of the will, by peopling the real with human works, by coloring the very resistance of reality with its patience as with its revolts." [6] Thus, in *L'homme faillible* Ricœur does what he points out here must be done, i.e., to restore the whole scope to the "giving of sense" which is consciousness in all its aspects.[7]

It is basically this difference with Husserl on the founded character of these other two spheres of consciousness, practical and affective, which is

[2] "Existential Phenomenology," p. 204.
[3] *Ibid.*
[4] Paul Ricœur, "Methods and Tasks," p. 221.
[5] *Ibid.*
[6] *Ibid.*
[7] *Ibid.*

at the root of the extension to reflective analysis on the practical and affective, opening up to the whole of the human and not limited to this
narrowness.[8] He indicates that we can develop the world-as-observed by
starting from the world of desiring or the world of *praxis*. Thus Ricœur
considers the voluntary life as yielding a privileged access to the problems
of constitution because . . ." consciousness is complete in one of its aspects;
it is human existence in its totality which in perceiving, willing, feeling,
imagining, etc., 'gives sense.' " [9]

Such an extension of turning to existence as *praxis* clears up certain
equivocations of sense-giving which cannot be raised to the level of the
theory of representation. "If we still wish to call transcendental the voluntary existence which institutes and discovers the practical aspects of the
world, such a transcendental cannot be considered creative. In fact the
signification of passivity remains hidden in a theory of representation." [10]

In his article on "Existential Phenomenology," Ricœur points out that
the method of existential phenomenology is that of transcendental phenomenology, but the problem set is that of existence.[11]

The idealistic tendency of transcendental phenomenology is "compen-
sated for by the progressive discovery that one does not constitute the
originary but only all that one can derive from it. And in a sense, all
phenomenology is transcendental, if by transcendental we mean "any attempt at relating the conditions of the appearance of things to the structure
of human subjectivity, in short to the very life of the subject to whom and
for whom things appear." [12]

We have already seen how Ricœur attempts to bring reflection to coincide with the revelation of the *pathétique* in his *L'homme faillible* in the
carrying out of this extension. However an absolute coincidence is impossible, and the reflection cannot actually become *pathétique*. Therefore,
a change of method is called for to compensate and to feed anew a further
path of enquiry. This has already been indicated as the hermeneutic path
which consists in interpreting the myths and symbols of avowal.[13]

DEEPENING TO EXPERIENCE

Ricœur makes an interesting observation in his article on existential phe-

[8] Paul Ricœur, "Methods and Tasks."
[9] *Ibid.*, p. 222.
[10] *Ibid.*
[11] Paul Ricœur, "Existential Phenomenology," p. 204.
[12] *Ibid.*
[13] Paul Ricœur, "Existence et Herméneutique," in *Interpretation der Welt.* ed. by
H. Kulm, H. Kahlefeld and K. Forster, p. 34.

nomenology. He says that "existential phenomenology makes the transition between transcendental phenomenology, born of the reduction of everything to its appearing to me, and ontology, which restores the question of the sense of being for all that is said to 'exist.' " [14] He considers this passing beyond the reflective mode of analysis to further fill the gap between the *pathétique* and the transcendental reflection, which calls for a different method, to be on the brink of ontology.[15] What this means is to some extent to release the phenomenological brackets of being, by admitting being into consideration, but not merely as such, at least not directly. Rather, phenomenology has its own way of eliciting the transition to the problem of being of the human existent by unveiling a specific non-being of the will, on the level or in the realm of a phenomenology of the will. "The privileged experience of this non-being, in spite of its negative turn, is already an ontological dimension; it is, so to speak, the negative proof of being, the empty ontology of lost being." [16] In its broadest sense this is a philosophical reflection on guilt which calls for the admitting of what he throughout his descriptive phenomenology has left bracketed out, i.e., a phenomenology of passion. The releasing of the brackets to allow a consideration of passion is actually a letting in of being, but under the guise of negation or non-being. Here we must review with him some considerations of passion, as he began in the first part of his philosophy of will, in the context of bracketing of fault. We must consider the relation of passion and guilt to non-being, and further elucidate this stage of phenomenology of the will.

When we considered Ricœur's abstraction from the passions above (chapters II & III) we did not see him disassociate them from the will. He makes it clear throughout that he does not consider them alien to the will. Rather, he considers them as the will itself, in its everyday, concrete real aspect. And that was the precise reason he spent so much time and effort to justify abstracting from them in the introduction to *Le volontaire et l'involontaire*. There the passions were seen as a "manner of being situated or of situating oneself, that inconsistent captivity is something entirely different from a complication of the involuntary, since it characterizes a way that the voluntary and the involuntary have of being a whole, a global image of existence." [17] Passion is considered an overall style, a kind of bondage which has its own intentionality, and all the intentionalities of

[14] Paul Ricœur, "Existential Phenomenology," p. 212.
[15] Paul Ricœur, "Methods and Tasks," p. 228.
[16] *Ibid.*
[17] *Ibid.*, p. 229.

partial functions are drawn along after it. Although the passions are the will itself in an alienated mode, we can however discover in every function of the involuntary the area of least resistance through which the passions enter and multiply.[18]

But once we take out of suspension the phenomenon of fault, the problem of guilt presents itself as a knot of impasses, which Ricœur finds necessary to discuss at some length in this context.[19] Since the passions are the everyday manifestation of willing, of which the voluntary and involuntary are still abstractions, they seem at first only to call for a description from ordinary observation, literature, and history, i.e., which would be an empirical description. However, the problem with that mode of access is that the passions have no principle of order in such manifestations needed to constitute a cosmos or ordered world, and thus lack an intelligibility.[20] And it seems that the myths of the fall, chaos, exile, etc.... cannot be inserted in their unrefined state into philosophical discourse. (HF, 10) We thus have to decipher the signs of each passion by the usages of life and culture, and so phenomenology comes up with the mythical character of the notion of guilt.[21]

The task of linking an empirics of the will to a mythics has been specified and expanded since Ricœur first wrote the introduction to *Le volontaire et l'involontaire.* There the idea of approaching the empirics of the will through a concrete mythics had already been formed, but he did not then fully realize the reasons for the turn. The question for him then was of the reason the passions which affect the will could only be spoken of in a coded language of a mythics or through their signs; and how to introduce this mythics into philosophic reflection; (HF, 10) and further, of how philosophical discourse could be resumed after such a detour or interruption by myth. However, by the time of *L'homme faillible* he sees this project of linking an empirics of the will to a mythics more clearly. (HF, 10)

The first task was to put the myths (those of fall, chaos, exile, and divine blinding) back into their universe of discourse, since they could not be inserted in their unrefined state in a philosophical discourse. It then became clear that myths could only be properly understood as a second level elaboration of primary symbols, that of a more fundamental language which Ricœur calls the language of avowal in *La symbolique du mal.* It is

---

[18] Paul Ricœur, "Methods and Tasks," p. 229.
[19] *Ibid.,* p. 229.
[20] *Ibid.*
[21] *Ibid.*

in this symbolics, on the level of symbols in the language of avowal, that the fault and evil reach the philosopher and speak to him. Therefore, to understand this language is to bring into play an exegesis of the symbol which calls for hermeneutics. "In this way the initial idea of a mythics of bad will has been expanded to the dimensions of a symbolics of evil." (HF, 10) Now the threefold structure of levels of the myth is made clear. In the center of this symbolics, we see the movement to what Ricœur calls the primary symbols. First of all, we must see that the most speculative expressions of the primary symbols are in expressions such as original sin, but that these most speculative are a third-level elaboration, which refer to mythic symbols. (HF, 10) These in turn refer to the more primary symbols, those of stain, sin, and guilt, treated in the initial part of *La symbolique du mal*. We shall leave for further discussion in the next part of this treatise the reasons and advantages of starting with these primary symbols.

La symbolique du mal therefore represents an enlargement of the mythics proposed by *Le volontaire et l'involontaire*. (HF, 11-12) The exegesis of its symbols prepares the myths for insertion into man's knowledge of himself. Ricœur points out in this context that the linguistic problems hold an important place. In fact the language of avowal is one of the enigmas of self-consciousness, since by it self-consciousness can only be expressed and reach its depth in riddles and requires a hermeneutics. (HF, 11)

The next and promised part of Ricœur's philosophy of the will is to be wholly devoted to thought which starts from the symbol. He says the rules for transposing it into a new type of philosophical discourse is outlined in the last chapter of *La symbolique du mal*: "The symbol gives rise to thought." It shows how we can think starting from the symbol. (HF, 12) He considers it as no longer possible today to "keep an empirics of the slave-will within the confines of a treatise on the passions in the Thomist, Cartesian or Spinozist fashion." (HF, 12) For a reflection on guilt doing justice to symbolic modes of expression we must encounter psychoanalysis. He also points out other directions this development must take. In order to make the symbolics of evil an empirics of the will, the evolution of criminology and conceptions of contemporary penal law come into play and consideration. (HF, 13) Also, we must not neglect political philosophy. We see here, therefore, the characteristics of the *thumos* analyzed in the later part of *L'homme faillible* coming up in their respective fields of empirical study, i.e., *avoir, pouvoir* and *valoir*.

"If 'The symbol gives rise to thought,' what the symbolics of evil gives to thought concerns the grandeur and limit of any ethical vision of the world, because the man who is revealed by this symbolics appears no less victim than guilty." (HF, 17) What Ricœur means here by the ethical is an attempt to understand freedom and evil by one another, which he has chosen in this part to do. (HF, 14)

The ultimate theme given over to thought by the symbolics is that riddle of the slave will, of a free will which is bound and always finds itself already bound. "It will be the task of philosophical reflection to take up again the suggestions of that symbolics of evil, to prolong them in every register of the consciousness of man, from the human sciences to speculation on the servile will." (HF, 17)

We have seen that the first impulse would have us simply look to ordinary observation, literature, and history for a description of the passions. However, we also saw how the passions lack an order principle, which they need, and so we need to decipher the signs of the passions by the usage of life and culture. We find also that the myth resists the tendency to a purely rational understanding, which reduces the myth to extract the purely rational understanding from it.[22] The myth resists because it alone has the power to bind sense (*Sinn*) and image (*Bild*) into an accident, a catastrophe, which would be a sort of transhistoric event of freedom; the event of the fall. Philosophy tends to reduce the event of guilt to a structure homogeneous with other structures of the voluntary and the involuntary, such as finitude as the ultimate philosophical alibi for guilt.[23] This is what Ricœur attempts to avoid by his access to the experience of evil through the myth and its hermeneutics, or that of the symbol underlying it:

The myth can thus serve as a heuristic guide for a description which otherwise would be in danger of indefinite dispersion into details. On the other hand, it is important to elaborate a philosophical critique of myth which would not be a reductive critique but would restore the significational intention of myth. The principal task of that critique is precisely to recapture the negative ontology of the notion of guilt, to disengage the specific sense of the "Powerful vanity," by showing the element which checks the attempt to reduce it to other modes of negativity (the experienced lack of need, the "always future emptiness" opened up before the self by the project, by the negation inherent in denial, and above all by the lack of aseity, that is by the non-necessity of the existing which is constitutive of finitude.[24]

What the bracketing of the passional modalities of the will has made possible is that it makes the willing and human existence in general appear as that which "gives sense." On the other hand, if reflection begins too

[22] Paul Ricœur, "Methods and Tasks," pp. 229-230.
[23] *Ibid.,* p. 230.
[24] *Ibid.,* p. 231.

soon with the passions, with "man's misery," it risks missing the signification of willing and of consciousness. Considering the notion of bondage too soon risks being confounded with a determinism or an automatism and would imprison anthropology in objective thought. "Thus, in order to disassociate the subjective world of motivation from the objective universe of causality, in order to regain the sense of spontaneity of the powers which the moving body offers for action, in order to regain, more subtly still, that necessity in the first person which I undergo simply by virtue of being alive, born of the flesh, phenomenology must organize that triple notion of motivation, spontaneity, and lived-through-necessity around a constitutive (or, in a limited sense, transcendental) "I will." To break through to that fundamental possibility of the ego which is its responsibility, Ricœur has suspended the bondage which oppresses the willing.[25] However, its suspension has allowed a reintroduction of it. And since he has been allowed by the commission of fault to see freedom as constitutive of involuntary, he considers servitude to be an accident of freedom.

However, to come to the "I will" in its constituting power, Ricœur has had to exclude the questions of the being and non-being of giving consciousness. "But then passing over into ontology would consist in dropping the parenthesis, and while keeping the advantages of the subjectivity acquired through use of the parenthesis, in attempting the adventure of a poiesis, of a 'poetics' of the will." [26]

TURN TO SYMBOLS

Ricœur's turn to symbolics of evil and to an hermeneutic of symbols is what we must take up now for consideration. Instead of beginning from an ontological point of view, with an ontological interpretation of the ontic to reach ontological conditions of man's being, he wishes to reach experience in a different manner. Ricœur wishes at this point to deal with the language of experience. On this level of experience, language becomes problematical, and also symbolic language of avowal. He is convinced that the experience of evil is spoken only in symbolic language, the language of avowal. This language is seen to be symbolic through and through, and so gives rise to an hermeneutics. Thus the symbolic structure becomes problematical, not only in this context of the symbols and myths of evil, but especially when this expression or use of the symbols is juxtaposed with

---

[25] Paul Ricœur, "Methods and Tasks," p. 232.
[26] *Ibid.*, p. 233.

other expressions or uses of symbols such as the symbols in psychoanalysis and poetry.

Thus the hermeneutic of Ricœur takes on a unique and new twist. His hermeneutic is not ontological in the same sense as Heidegger's, and deals with experience in a different way. Heidegger begins with the ontic, with empirical man. His access to the explicit meaning of Being, to the hermeneutical circle, is to enter or begin with the analysis of man's everyday being, and to explicitate its essential structures, its existentiality, so that, by means of an hermeneutics in the sense of letting Being manifest itself in man, he wishes to come to or explicitate the pre-conceptual comprehension of the Being of man, and so the explicit meaning of Being.

Ricœur wishes to take particular, achieved hermeneutics of experience. He wishes in that manner to work toward ontology. He is committed to the primacy of Being, but works from experience through these various hermeneutics to ontology. Since he has bracketed the fault from eidetics, and has not considered man's concrete condition, since the existential level of *L'homme faillible* has only localized the existential possibility of evil in man, he still must consider the concrete fallen man, the innocent man, and the transition from innocence to fault. None of these can be arrived at above the level of experience, and can be obtained only through their symbolic expressions.

One of the basic questions for this study is exactly what kind of access to experience is this. What does it tell us about man's being that an ontological hermeneutic which moves directly from the ontic to the ontological misses. Is it really worth all the trouble to engage in such a laborious toil as the conflict in interpreting the same symbols in their relevancy to a philosophical anthropology? This is not a proposal to discuss or defend Ricœur's ontology, but to follow him along his path and make explicit the extensions and developments later places on the path require of the earlier.

Thus the basic crux of this study emerges. The basic problem focuses on Ricœur's turn to experience or to the ontic by a turn to symbolic expressions in which experience is expressed, instead of turning directly to the ontic, everyday existence of man, in a movement from pre-comprehension to conceptual comprehension of the meaning of Being.

The first discussion of the next chapters of this treatise will discuss the phenomenology and philosophy of language to show how experience is expressed. The structure of symbolic expressions will be analyzed epistemologically or transcendentally. Since symbolic structure allows for the expression of accidental aspects of man's being, such as fault, guilt, innocence, the transition from innocence to guilt, its advantages or yield must be borne out to some extent. We shall therefore have to investigate Ricœur's initial theory of symbols as it unfolds in this first confrontation with the symbols of evil, and with the different modes of interpreting them. This finally, as we shall see, leads into a deeper and extended philosophy of language, especially after he explicitly focuses on the semiological sciences.

CHAPTER V

SYMBOL, HERMENEUTIC AND CONFLICT
OF INTERPRETATION

INTRODUCTION

The last three chapters were an attempt to characterize the eidetic level of pure reflection in Ricœur's philosophical investigations on the will and to make the transition to concrete reflection.

The beginning of this chapter must make the transition to the hermeneutical level of interpreting concrete symbols. The title of a couple of his essays in *Le Conflit des interprétations* is significant in relation to this transition to the concrete man. In these essays, especially the second, we can see the articulation of the problems confronted by the philosopher in confronting symbols and hermeneutics; the conflict among interpretations in the same field of hermeneutics. It is this same conflict which gives Ricœur the title to his whole collection of essays. The second of these essays in this book under the same title, and numbered as "II," is almost a verbatim presentation of the *Terry Lectures* of Ricœur given at Yale University in 1961.[1] This is also the article first published under the title "Herméneutique et Réflexion" in *Demitizzazione e imagine* (Actes du Congrès international, Rome).

The important point is that these *Terry Lectures* or this article which is at the origin of the investigations begun at this time on Freud, also gave rise to *De l'interprétation*. (DI, 7) And after this delving into the philosophical implication of Freud and the detour into semiology, he initiates further investigations on the sciences of language and the general view of sign.

Thus the purpose of this chapter becomes clear. This chapter must be a passage from the levels of pure reflection to the hermeneutical level of the philosophy of the will. In the first level, the foundation was being laid for a fundamental *thématique* on the problem of evil. But it was in the manner

[1] DI, 7. Here Ricœur tells of the origin of the book from those lectures.

of a necessary prolegomenon (VI, 36) and therefore does not make this problem explicitly thematic. It merely considers its essential and its existential possibility in the structures of man's willing. On that level it was necessary to bracket out the fault and the concrete man as such, i.e., the fallen (and innocent) aspect of man. It is this character of man's fallenness which the hermeneutical level wishes to capture. Therefore it begins by treating the symbols and myths of evil, which Ricœur has become convinced are the access to the expressions of the concrete experience of evil.

La symbolique du mal therefore is the beginning of hermeneutics for Ricœur. He begins first by investigating the primary symbols which he found to underlie the mythical level as their second level. Then he considers these primary symbols as they are carried into more elevated expressions in the myths of evil. The third level to which they are carried he considers in some of the essays and lectures amassed in *Le conflit des interprétations*.

Even though Ricœur's first work in his hermeneutical phenomenology of the will is *La symbolique du mal,* we shall not begin with it. Instead, since our interest is chiefly his transition to this level of reflection, and the problems which he must confront on this level, and the possible extensions these confrontations might make necessary in the prior levels, we shall begin with a consideration of his theory of interpretation and symbols. Thus we continue the line of development outlined in the first chapter of this treatise.

Such a consideration of the structure of symbolic expression and the hermeneutics of symbols naturally leads to the conflict of interpretations within the same hermeneutic field. From the nature of this conflict it becomes clear to Ricœur that he must confront Freudian interpretation as anti-phenomenological with phenomenology. This confrontation with Freud and with semiology in general will be discussed as a necessary confrontation for Ricœur, springing from the findings in the first hermeneutics of the symbols of evil in *La symbolique du mal,* and springing from his decision to take the long way to a general hermeneutics of the "I am" and to ontology in order that he might confront this problem. He has chosen to meet the difficulty presented by several already practiced hermeneutic methods. (CI, 14) Thus he has remained constant in his attempt to make philosophy the arbitrator with the sciences. Just as he uses the sciences in *Le volontaire et l'involontaire* and *L'homme faillible,* he wants to accept the results of the sciences for philosophy but in a critical manner and without compromising the phenomenological insight of intentionality or reference and self-imputation or reference to a self. In this manner he endeavors to open the closed perspectives of the sciences.

SYMBOL

In beginning both his *De l'interprétation* and *La symbolique du mal*, Ricœur uses a brief eidetic description in imaginative variation to come up with a definition of symbols and hermeneutics, which he tersely recounts in "Existence et Hermeneutique." (CI, 16) In this article he follows closely his manner of treatment of *De l'interprétation*, in which he defines symbol and interpretation in their relation to one another, thus limiting one by the other. His procedure of treatment is similar in each case. He contrasts narrow and broad uses or definitions of each, and defines the way he takes both symbol and interpretation as intermediary between these extremes. (DI, 18) Symbols, therefore, are situated between the symbolic function the way Cassirer develops it, and Aristotle's doctrine of analogy.[2] Our concern for the purpose of this chapter will be with Ricœur's treatment of symbol and interpretation rather than with his eidetic descriptions.

The most general delineation of the symbol is that it is a sign. As such it is an expression which communicates a meaning. But this is too broad. Every symbol is a sign, but not every sign is a symbol. What characterizes a sign as a symbol for Ricœur is the double meaning, or the double intentionality which the symbol conceals in its aim.[3] This is the intentional structure of the symbol, which is so important for Ricœur, and especially relevant to his theory of interpretation, since it gives rise to the need for interpretation. There is the literal intentionality which implies the triumph of the conventional over the natural sign. The second intentionality to which he refers is built upon this first intentionality, which points to the second. This second intentionality is not given except in the first, the literal, patent meaning.[4]

For Ricœur, this duality of the symbolic function must be distinguished from the duality of the sensible sign and its signification, and from the signification and the thing or the object designated. (DI, 21) The symbol presupposes the signs which already have a primary, literal, manifest sense, and which, by this sense, returns to another sense. He deliberately restricts

---

[2] Although Ricœur later extends these views regarding symbols and interpretation, we shall remain true to these earlier investigations, leaving the explicit treatment of his later views for the following chapters.

[3] SM, p. 21-22; "The Hermeneutics of Symbols and Philosophical Reflection," *IPQ,* vol. 2, p. 194; DI, p. 18.

[4] *Ibid.*

the notion of symbol to the expressions with a double sense. The semantic texture of these is correlative to the work of interpretation which explicates its second sense. (DI, 21)

Thus it is not difficult to arrive at Ricœur's definition of symbols. "I call symbol every structure of signification in which a direct, primary, literal sense designates by excess another sense, indirect, secondary, figured, which cannot be apprehended except across the first." (CI, 16) This definition captures to some extent what Ricœur speaks of as the common structure of symbols.

Ricœur distinguishes the analogous bond between the literal and the symbolic meaning from the analogy as a reasoning process through a fourth proportional term.[5] In the symbolic structure, the analogous relation which binds the second meaning to the first cannot be objectivated. By living in the first meaning I am drawn by it beyond itself. The symbolic meaning is constituted in and through the literal meaning. Symbol is the movement of the primary meaning that makes us share in the latent meaning and thus assimilates us to the symbolized without our being able to intellectually dominate the similarity. This for Ricœur is one sense in which the symbol "gives"; it gives because it is a primary intentionality that gives the second meaning.

Ricœur takes a particular interest in the epistemology of the symbol, especially with regard to its common structure. In his book on Freud he is especially interested in the epistemology of the symbol or its common structure in the different modes of the symbol's emergence. (DI, 23) He is looking for the texture of the symbol common to all symbols, to all these zones of emergence, rather than only a particular mode of manifestation, as was done in *La symbolique du mal*. He will therefore treat the double meaning or the double intentional structure, attempting to base it transcendentally. This step is essential to the development or movement to ontology.

Zones of emergence

Ricœur indicates that if we go beneath the more elaborated symbols which are already on the road of reflection, such as the moral or tragic vision, we find three zones or modalities of manifestation of symbols. The unity of these different manifestations is not immediately visible. (DI, 23)

1. The first manifestation is the phenomenology of religion, such as those of Van der Leeuw, Maurice Leenhardt, and Mircea Eliade. These

[5] SM, p. 22; DI, p. 22; "Hermeneutics of Symbols," p. 194.

symbols are bound to the rites and to the myths, constituting the language of the sacred, the word of the Hierophanies. They treat symbolism of the heaven, as figure of the very high and of the immense, of the power and of the immutable, of the sovereign and of the wise, etc. . . . It is in the universe of discourse that these realities take the symbolic dimension. Even when these are the elements of the universe which carry the symbol, – Heaven, Earth, Water, Life, etc., it is the word which says the cosmic expressibility by means of the double sense of the words: earth, heaven, water, life, etc. The expressibility of the world comes to language by the symbol as double sense. (DI, 23)

2. The second zone of emergence of the symbol or manifestation is that of the *onérique,* or the dreams of our days and of our nights. It is the dream which attests to the fact that we wish to say something other than what we say. There is the manifest sense which incessantly goes back to a hidden sense and makes a poet of the dreamer. (DI, 24)

The mythic and oneric have in common this structure of the double sense. The dream as a nocturnal spectacle is unknown to us. In fact, it is accessible to us only at the recital of the person once he is awakened. It is the dream as spoken, as recited, which the analyst interprets. (DI, 24)

3. For Ricœur, the third zone of emergence or manifestation of the symbol is that of the poetic imagination. He points out that it is the least understood without the detour of the cosmic and of the *onérique.* (DI, 24) The imagination has been too quickly spoken of as the power of the images; this is not true if we understand by image the representation of an absent or unreal thing, a procedure to render present, to make present, the thing over there, moreover, or not at all. The poetic imagination is not at all reduced to this power to form a mental portrait of the unreal. The imagery of the sensorial origin serves only as a vehicle and material for the verbal power of which the oneric and the cosmic render the true dimension. As Bachelard says, the poetic image "puts us at the origin of the speaking being"; the poetic image, he says again, "becomes a new being of our language. It expresses us in making us what it expresses." That verb-image which traverses the image-representation is the symbol. (DI, 24-25)

In all three cases of the emergence of the symbol the problem of the symbol is the same, or resolves itself into the problem of language. There is no *symbolique* before the man who speaks, even if the power of the symbol is rooted at a more basic level, in the expressibility of the cosmos, in the *vouloir-dire* of the desire, in the imaginative variety of the subjects. "But each time it is in language that the cosmos, desire, the imagination come to the word." (DI, 25) It is the poet who shows us the birth of the word, such that it was unfolded in the enigmas of the cosmos and of the psyche. The force of the poet is to show the symbol at the moment when the rite and the myth fix it in its stability and where the dream closes it on the labyrinth of desire in which the dreamer looses the string of his forbidden and mutilated discourse. (DI, 25)

In these various zones of emergence of the symbol, Ricœur takes the double meaning or the double intentional structures as their common structure. He says that he defines symbol by a common semantic structure, that of the double sense, in order to give consistence and unity to these scattered manifestations. "There is a symbol when language produces signs of composed degree in which the sense, not content with designating something, designates another sense which would be attained only in and by its aim." (DI, 25)

We have seen that there is a symbol where the linguistic expression readies itself by a double sense or its multiple senses for the work of interpretation. That which raises this work is an intentional structure which does not consist in the relation of sense to the thing, but in an architecture of the sense, in a relation of sense to sense, of a second sense to a first sense. It is that texture which renders possible the interpretation, although only the movement effective of interpretation renders it manifest. (DI, 26)

For Ricœur it is by its exigency of interpretation that the problem of symbol inscribes itself in the more broad problem of language. For this bond to interpretation is not exterior to the symbol. The symbol is an enigma in the Greek sense of the word, but this enigma does not block understanding. Rather, it provokes it. It is precisely the double sense, the intentional aim of the second sense in and by the first which raises the understanding; in the figured expressions of the servile will which constitute the symbol of confession, Ricœur admits he was able to show that it is the very surcharge of sense, by relation to the literal expression, which puts the interpretation into movement. (DI, 27)

INTERPRETATION

Ricœur considers interpretation, therefore, as belonging organically to symbolic thought and to its double sense. (DI, 27) This is why, as has been said above, he attempts to limit one by the other, so that in discussing the symbol and its structure, the need for interpretation comes to light. We have seen how the need for the interpretation of the double sense of the symbol's intentional structure arises from the very nature of the symbol.

Ricœur proceeds here in much the same fashion as he did in delineating the definition of symbol. He first opposes himself to the too broad view of interpretation of Aristotle,[6] then to the too narrow view of Scriptural exegesis, and places himself or his view somehow in the middle. Aristotle's view, with his use of analogy and *pros hen* equivocals, is too broad. The Biblical limits hermeneutics by exegesis, by its reference to an authority. (DI, 29)

Ricœur sometimes speaks of hermeneutics or interpretation as an exegesis. (DI, 35) However, we must not misunderstand him. He has in mind an enlarged concept of exegesis which consists of rules or the science of rules of exegesis. But we have to see that the text can be broader than is usually taken in a more narrow acceptance of exegesis. The text can be every ensemble of signs susceptible of being considered as a text to be deciphered, such as a dream, a nervous symptom, a rite, a myth, a work of art, a belief. (DI, 35)

Conflict of interpretations

The main difficulty which has interested Ricœur is that there is not a general hermeneutic, not a universal canon for the exegesis, but separate and opposed theories concerning the rules of interpretation. The hermeneutic field is broken. (DI, 35) On the one hand, hermeneutics is conceived as the manifestation and the restoration of a sense which is addressed to me in the manner of a message, of a proclamation, or as is sometimes said, of a Kerygma; on the other hand, it is conceived as a demystification, as a reduction of illusions. It is from this side of the fight that psychoanalysis places itself, at least in the first reading. (DI, 35-36) These two hermeneutics set up the most extreme tension. Ricœur places himself here in the midst of this most extreme tension so that he will not have to go through the many types of exegesis or hermeneutics. (DI, 36)

The opposition clearly becomes more extreme as Ricœur draws out the main traits of each type and opposes the traits of the one to those of the other. One of these interpretations is that of an exercise of suspicion; the other opposed to it is faith. It is not the first naive faith, but rather that second faith of the hermeneutist, the faith which has traversed the critique, the post-critical faith. It is a reasonable faith because it interprets, but it is a faith because it looks for, by the interpretation, a second naiveté. For it phenomenology is the instrument of hearing, of recollection, of restoration of sense. To believe to understand, to understand to believe, such is its

---

[6] This view is later extended and Ricœur will end up having to qualify this earlier position.

maxim; and its maxim is the hermeneutical circle itself of believing and understanding. (DI, 37)

Ricœur attempts to unfold the reasonable faith which traverses the purely intentional analysis of the religious symbolism and which converts from within this analysis in hearing. (DI, 37) We can consider these three traits,[7] or the main presuppositions of the phenomenology of religion, which can be opposed to three traits of psychoanalysis. The last book of *De l'interprétation* deals with each of these traits in turn.

1. In pointing out and elucidating what he considers this first trait, Ricœur begins with the very foundation or basis of this phenomenology, the distinction between describing and explaining.[8] This brings out the phenomenologists' care of the object, characteristic of all phenomenological analysis.

He does not mean to belittle the genetic or the explanation which tries to understand the ultimate forms as complicated forms of more simple forms. Rather, explanation in terms of function or source or origin does not mean we have really understood the phenomena. What he proposes is to describe the phenomena, beginning with the object, or with the care of the object. "To describe is to refer the religious phenomenon to its object, such as it is intended and such as it is given in the cult and in the belief, in rite and myth." [9] (p. 6, Terry L. 1) This description proceeds by disengaging the aim (noetic) and its correlate (noematic), which is the something aimed at, the object implicit in the rite, in the myth and in the belief. Instead of the cause, the genesis, the simpler form, the object is the guide for Ricœur in gaining access to the genuine comprehension of the intentional aim.[10] (Terry L. 1, p. 6)

This care of the object as the first trait of a phenomenology brings out Ricœur's movement in this phenomenology from the literal meaning of symbols to the latent, hidden meaning. If we focus with him on his analysis of the pure and impure, we can see with him that the task is to understand what is meant, what is signified, what quality of the sacred is aimed at, "what nuance of threat is implied in that analogy between the stain and defilement, between physical contamination and the loss of existential integrity." (DI, 37) This care of the object was for Ricœur the docility to

---

[7] DI, pp. 37-40; this discussion will follow the traits laid down both in this section of DI, and in Ricœur's Terry Lecture of 1961. The discussion of the traits opposed to those of the phenomenology of religion are more easily discussed from the Terry Lectures.

[8] Paul Ricœur, *First Terry Lecture*, p. 6.

[9] *Ibid.*, p. 6.

[10] *Ibid.*

the movement of the sense which, beginning with the literal signification, the stain, contamination, points toward the seizing of something in the region of the sacred. To generalize the theme of the phenomenology of religion for Ricœur, we can say that it is the something aimed at in the ritual action, in the mythic word, in the faith or the mystic sentiment; its task is to desimplify that "object" of diverse intentions from conduct, from discourse, and from emotion. He therefore calls "sacred" that object aimed at, without prejudicing its nature. (DI, 37)

Here Ricœur brings up a fundamental difficulty pervading all his phenomenology, distinguishing him from many other phenomenologists, at least in the way he eventually attempts to solve it. The problem deals with the *epoché,* and being which it attempts to bracket. Ricœur in the context we have been elaborating upon, expresses the problem as to whether the phenomenology of the "sacred" can remain within the limits of a neutral attitude, one which is ruled by the *epoché,* by putting between parentheses the absolute reality and all questions concerning the absolute. The *epoché* for him demands that I participate in the belief in the reality of the religious object, but in a neutralized mode; that I believe with the believer, but without posing absolutely the object of his belief. (DI, 38)

But even so, for Ricœur the philosopher cannot just avoid the question of the absolute validity of this object. If the first trait is the care of the object, if there is such an interest in the object, is there not also a confidence that the object will somehow speak to me? In thus waiting for the object, does this not express also a confidence in the language which carries the symbols as speaking to me. (DI, 38) For Ricœur therefore, the language of avowal which carried the symbol is a word to men, and in the midst of which man is born. This we will see is the point of emergence of being, since this word is a word of being, for Ricœur, as well as for Heidegger. It is the word of being which speaks to man, emerges within man, who is born in its midst. For Ricœur therefore, being is not from the middle of man, but contrary-wise, man is in the midst of being.

This recourse to language or to the symbol as speaking to man is contested by the whole current of hermeneutics which Ricœur calls suspicious. This begins with the doubt that there is such an object and that that object can be the place of the inversion of the intentional aim in Kerygma, in manifestation and in proclamation. It is why that hermeneutic is not disillusionment of the object, reductive interpretation of disguises. (DI, 38)

2. Second trait: the truth of symbols. Ricœur points out that he is taking this truth of the symbol in much the same way Husserl in his *Logical Investigations* understands fulfillment, i.e., *die Erfüllung,* the fulfillment of

the signifying intention, of the meaningful intention.[11] Ricœur proposes to treat this problem by focusing on the union, the bond between the first, primary, literal sense and the second sense. He begins with the opposition between sign and symbol, just as he did before with the opposition between understanding by the object and explanation by the cause, function or origin.

For Ricœur it is in that bond or liaison of the sense to the sense that resides what he has called the fullness of language which is so important for his symbolics and for his starting point of reflection. (DI, 39) This fullness of language means that the second sense lives in the first sense in some way. Mircea Eliade shows well that the force of the cosmic symbolism resides in the bond which is not arbitrary between the visible heaven and the order which it manifests; he speaks of the wise and of the just, of the immense and of the ordered, that is, of the analogical power which binds the sense to the sense. The symbol is bound, as we have seen above, and bound in a double sense: bound to and bound by. On the other hand, the literal signification is bound by the symbolic sense which resides in it. It is what Ricœur has called the revealing power of the symbol, that makes up its force despite its opacity. It is that which opposes it to the technical sign which signifies nothing more than what is posited there and which, for that reason, can be emptied, formalized and reduced to a simple object of calculus. Only the symbol gives what it says. (DI, 39)

Thus we can see that at this stage, Ricœur has separated himself from those who over-extend the meaning of the symbolic function to mean almost or exactly the same thing as the signifying function. The symbol has the characteristic of not being so arbitrary; it is not empty, since there is always a natural relation between the signifying and the signified, as we have seen above.[12]

Ricœur admits and even emphasizes, as he did with regard to the first trait, that this trait, beginning with the full of language, infringes on the phenomenological neutrality. He admits that "what motivates in depth that interest for the full language, for the bound language, is that inversion of movement of thought which addresses itself to me and makes me an interpellated subject." [13] And that inversion is produced in analogy. The question, as he poses it, is one of how that which binds the sense to the sense binds me. It binds me because the movement which drags me toward the second sense assimilates me to that which is said, renders me partici-

---

[11] Paul Ricœur, *First Terry Lecture,* pp. 7-8; DI, pp. 38-39.
[12] Paul Ricœur, *First Terry Lecture,* pp. 8-9.
[13] *Ibid.*

pating in that which is announced to me. The similitude in which resides the force of the symbol and of which the symbol draws its revealing power is not in effect an objective resemblance, that I could consider as a relation exposed before me; it is rather an existential assimilation of my beginning to being according to the movement of analogy.[14]

3. Third trait: Ontological bearing of these symbols of the Sacred. This third trait has been hinted at in the other two, which would take the symbols as the word of Being, following Heidegger's philosophy of language.[15] We have seen how the other traits of symbols in phenomenology of religion have led to this point of language also. For Ricœur this philosophy of language is implicit in the phenomenology of religion. As phenomenology, in using the *epoché,* I must live in the belief, in the reality of the object, but only in a neutralized mode. However, I cannot avoid the question of the absolute validity of the object. For Ricœur it is at this point that the philosophy of language of Heidegger meets the phenomenology of religion, proclaiming that the full language is the language of Being, that this language is less spoken by men than spoken to men, that men were born in the bosom of language.[16] He focuses on the full language, and the analogy which links the signifying to the signified. It is in that likeness that the strength of the symbol abides and draws its revealing power. Ricœur contrasts this as the *analogia entis* to the *via negativa.*[17] Speaking of this *analogiae via,* he likes to refer to it as a modern version of ancient reminiscence.[18] The modern care for the symbol expresses a new desire to be interpellated, beyond that silence and forgetting which makes the manifestation of empty signs and the construction of formalized language to proliferate.[19]

"That awaiting of a new word, of a new actuality of the word, is the implicit thought of all phenomenology of symbols, which puts first the accent on the object, then underlines the fullness of the symbol, in order finally to welcome the revealing power of the original word."[20]

To these three traits of the phenomenology of religion Ricœur opposes three traits of psychoanalysis. As we have seen, his intention is to take the tension between the conflicting interpretations or manners of interpretation

---

[14] Paul Ricœur, *First Terry Lecture,* pp. 8-9.
[15] *Ibid.,* p. 10.
[16] *Ibid.,* pp. 10-11.
[17] *Ibid.*
[18] *Ibid.,* p. 11; DI, p. 40; "Hermeneutics of Symbols," p. 194.
[19] *Ibid.*
[20] *Ibid.*

at its most extreme opposition. Each of these manners of interpretation has its own manner of viewing symbols. It is necessary now to follow Ricœur as he draws out three contrary or opposed traits of symbols, those of psychoanalysis diametrically opposed to those already discussed. Ricœur opposes these two interpretations as on the one hand, that which restores the sense, and on the other hand, that which he calls the school of suspicion, that of Nietzsche, Marx, and Freud. (DI, 40)

It is necessary now to follow Ricœur as he discusses the three counter traits of psychoanalysis. To the objective interpretation of religion in phenomenology, psychoanalysis opposes the functional interpretation of religion; to the truth of symbols in the sense of their fullness, psychoanalysis opposes the idea of illusion; and finally to the "reminiscence of the Sacred," that of the theme of the "return of the repressed." [21]

1. First Trait: religion as a function of culture. Opposed to the objectival approach of phenomenology of religion, Ricœur sees Freud opposing a religion as function of religion in civilization. It is for Freud within a dynamics of civilization that we have to understand religion. Psychoanalysis has the ultimate intention to be general hermeneutics of culture, and it is not confined to a diagnosis and healing of mental disease. Psychoanalysis that belongs to our culture as one of the means by which this culture reflects upon itself and understands itself. Therefore it extends to the same field as other hermeneutics, as a global interpretation of civilization. Each of these wishes to grasp the whole of man to interpret and understand the whole of man.[22]

Since it extends to all civilization and the whole of man, psychoanalysis is limited not by its objects, but by its point of view. Its point of view is that of an economy of impulses, i.e., of a balance of renouncements and gratifications. And this economic point of view can be understood only in relation to the dynamic and topographical points of view.[23]

2. Second Trait: theory of illusion. This second trait of psychoanalysis is opposed to phenomenology of religion in its theory of truth or fulfillment. What is new in this theory of illusion of Freud's is that this is an economic interpretation of illusion. The question here is that of the function of religious representations in the balance of renouncements and of the gratifications or compensations through which man attempts to endure life. The key is the hardness of life which is hard to endure, especially for a being eager for consolation because of inborn narcissism. Civili-

[21] Paul Ricœur, *First Terry Lecture*, p. 13.
[22] *Ibid.*, pp. 13-14.
[23] *Ibid.*, p. 14.

zation must reduce the instincts, but in addition it must defend man against the overwhelming superiority of nature. Illusion is another means that civilization uses when the struggle against nature fails. It invests the gods to get rid of fear, to reconcile man with the cruelty of fate and to compensate for the discontents made incurable by the death instinct.[24]

Ricœur now focuses on a fundamental problem of this economical function of religion as illusion, or this economical function of illusion; that presented by the idea of an economical interpretation of a representation. It would seem at first that such an economical interpretation would deal only with forces, impulses, with their cathexis, withdrawal of cathexis, counter-cathexis. This problem is solved for Freud, it seems, by the assumption that between impulses and representations exists a primordial connection. Ricœur interprets the naked impulses as the thing-in-itself of psychoanalysis, which it does not deal with as such, but rather with their representative ideas. This is the reason psychoanalysis deals with phantasms, images, symbols, myths. These impulses, or the things-in-themselves of psychonalysis, are never reached as such an their representations are reached in their presentations.[25] The illusion thus can be understood as a particular case of "substitutive formations and symptoms which manifest derivates of the unconscious at the level of consciousness.[26]

3. Third trait: genesis of religious illusion. It is at this level of the third trait, or of the ontological bearing of the symbol, that Ricœur sees the most extreme discrepancy between psychoanalysis and phenomenology.[27] We saw how he treated in this trait of phenomenology of religion the ontological bearing of symbol, the interpretation of the symbolism of the Sacred appearing as a renewal of the ancient Reminiscence. He juxtaposes a Reminiscence in psychoanalysis. Here however, this reminiscence is a genesis of the religious illusion, starting from the symbols and the phantasms in which the earliest conflicts of ancient men and of infants are expressed. This is the moment of merging of the genetic explanation into the topographical and economic explanation. If religious representations are mere illusions, they can only be understood through their origin.[28]

There are two elements important in the procedure: the return to the past and the return long after of what has been forgotten. This latter, too long overlooked, can be compared for Freud to the return of the repressed in obsessional neurosis. Thus we see the parallelism he draws between

[24] Paul Ricœur, *First Terry Lecture*, pp. 16-17.
[25] *Ibid.*, p. 18.
[26] *Ibid.*
[27] *Ibid.*
[28] *Ibid.*, pp. 18-19.

Jewish monotheism and traumatic neurosis; Ricœur quotes a passage of Freud to show this: [29]

... early trauma-defense-latency- outbreak of the neurosis – partial return of the repressed material: this was the formula for the development of any neurosis (in the same way) mankind as a whole also passed through conflicts of a sexual-aggressive nature, which left permanent traces, but were chiefly warded off and forgotten, only much later after a period of latency, to come to life again . . . . .

He adds by way of commentary on this passage, "In this way the etiology of neurosis complements the genetic explanation which in its turn completes the functional and economic explanation of religious phenomena." This comparison gives us another glance at the split in the field of hermeneutics. "Reminiscence of the Sacred in the sense of an ontology of symbols, return of the repressed in the sense of an etiology of phantasms constitute the two poles of the tension in the field of hermeneutics." [30]

These two systems of interpretation reveal the extreme tension between the traits of each as opposed to those of the other. However it is necessary to realize that it is the same symbols which feed these conflicting manners of interpreting, because of their structure as bearing two dimensions or vectors.[31]

Springing from the same symbols, these two sciences of interpretation are two opposed movements. The one is progressive, synthetic, revealing of meaning; the other is regressive, analytical, attempting to uncover illusion.[32] For Ricœur, it is the mind that is the order of the ultimate, and the unconscious that is the order of the primeval.

REFLECTION

It is necessary to notice an essential transition in the working out of Ricœur's hermeneutics. For Ricœur the comprehension of the symbols as expressions with double meanings is a moment of the comprehension of the self, so that the semantic approach is chained to a reflective approach. (CI, 15-20) This means that he wishes to graft hermeneutics onto phenomenology at the level of the *Cogito* as well as at the level of meaning. And just as his view of symbols as multivocal expression calls for a radical change from Husserl's univocal expressions, this latter place of grafting, the *Cogito,* undergoes radical modification. "The subject which is inter-

---

[29] Paul Ricœur, *First Terry Lecture,* pp. 20-21.
[30] *Ibid.,* pp. 20-21.
[31] Paul Ricœur, *Second Terry Lecture,* pp. 10-12, 21.
[32] *Ibid.,* p. 11.

preted in interpreting the signs is no longer the *Cogito,* but rather an existent, who discovers by the exegesis of his life that it is posited in being before even it posits itself and possesses itself." (CI, 39)

The transitions to be considered are: first, the transition from semantics to reflection; and second, that from reflection to existence and ontology. Our concern now is with the need for reflection on the part of the symbol and the need of reflection for the symbol and interpretation. This discussion will mainly follow Ricœur's discussion in *De l'interprétation* since this is his clearest expression of the relation of mutual need between the semantic and reflection. (DI, 45-63)

This is a most critical stage of development in Ricœur's philosophy, for it has to do with the working toward a starting point in the full language and with the archeology of the subject.

For Ricœur philosophy does not begin anything from nothing. Rather, the full of language precedes it, and in a way, as we have already discussed it in chapter four, says everything before philosophy begins. The symbol, however, is the gift of language to thought and gives rise to the duty to think, to begin philosophical discourse from what already goes before it. Thus the symbol demands reflection. The symbol frames an appeal not only to inter-pretation, but also to philosophical reflection. (DI, 46)

On the level of the first demand of the symbol for reflection in *La symbolique du mal,* the semantic structure gives rise to or needs interpre-tation and so demands reflection. However, the purely semantic aspect was seen to be not the only aspect but only the most abstract. These linguistic expressions in *La symbolique du mal* are seen to be incorporated not only in the rites and the emotions but also in myths. This is the second appeal to reflection of the symbol. (DI, 46)

Ricœur sees in this second level of symbols, that of myth, a further call for reflection by a demand for interpretation. On this level, new traits of the symbol appear, and with them, new suggestions for a hermeneutics. These myths as a spoken recital recount, in the manner of a transhistoric event, the irrational rupture, the absurd blow, which separates two con-fessions bearing, one on the innocence of the future and the other on the culpability of history; on this level, the symbols not only have a semantic but also a heuristic value because they confer universality, temporality, and ontological bearing on the comprehension of ourselves. Interpretation does not now consist simply in the *dégagement* of the second intention, which is at the same time given and masked in the literal sense; it attempts to make thematic that universality, that temporality, that ontological ex-ploration implicated in the myth. Ricœur is led to conclude that it is the symbol itself which, under the mythic form, pushes toward speculative expression; it is the symbol itself which is the dawn of reflection. (DI, 46-47) Since it is the symbol itself which is the dawn of reflection, the hermeneutic problem can be seen as not imposed from outside on reflection but proposed from within by the very movement of sense, by the implicit life of the symbols taken on their semantic level and mythic level. (DI, 47)

There is yet a third manner in which *La symbolique du mal* makes an appeal to a science of interpretation, to an hermeneutic. Both on the semantic and on the mythic level, the symbols of evil are opposite to a more vast symbolism, that of a symbolism of salvation. It is this symbolism of salvation which confers its true meaning on the symbolism of evil. This latter is only one interior province at the interior of a religious symbolism. Ricœur is able to clarify this position by pointing out that the Christian Creed says, "I believe in the remission of sins," and not "I believe in sin." This correspondence between the symbolism of evil and salvation signifies that it is necessary to go beyond our fascination for a symbolism of evil cut off from the rest of the symbolic and mythic universe and to reflect on the totality which these symbols form with the commencement and the end. This suggests the architectonic task of reason, already designated in the play of mythic correspondences. It is that totality as such which demands to be said on the level of reflection and of speculation. (DI, 42-48)

After thus considering the demand of the symbol at each level for reflection, Ricœur poses the other side of the problem: How can a philosophy of reflection be fed on a symbolic source and become hermeneutical? (DI, 48)

Thus reflective philosophy, which Ricœur likes to call philosophical science, is presented with somewhat of a scandal in its recourse to symbols. The first reason for this scandal is that the symbol remains the prisoner of the diversity of languages and of cultures and espouses irreducible singularity for them. It is now my singularity which I put at the center of my reflection; but philosophical science should need a reabsorption of singularity of cultural creations and of individual memories in the universality of discourse. (DI, 49)

Secondly, philosophy as science demands univocal significations, but the symbol is opaque, non-transparent, concrete, constitutive, existential; and that opacity can only wish to bespeak equivocity. (DI, 49)

Thirdly, every interpretation is revocable. The bond between the symbol and interpretation, in which we have seen the promise of an organic liaison between myth and *logos,* furnishes a new motif of suspicion. No mythic without exegesis, but no exegesis without contestation. The deciphering of enigmas is not a science. The task is not only to justify the recourse to some genre of interpretation but to justify the dependence of reflection on already constituted hermeneutics which mutually exclude one another. (DI, 49)

Thus for Ricœur, to justify the recourse to symbolism in philosophy is finally to justify the cultural contingency, equivocal language, and the war of hermeneutics in the very bosom of reflection. This problem will be resolved if one arrives at showing that reflection in its very principle demands something like interpretation. It is beginning from this exigency that the detour by cultural contingency, by an incurably equivocal language and by the conflict of interpretations, can be justified. (DI, 50)

Resolution of Conflict of Interpretation

Ricœur states that the resolution of the conflict between the two opposed types of interpretation grounded in reflection is in the dialectic of archeology and teleology. (DI, 476) But before discussing this dialectic, it is necessary to articulate briefly the other two phases: before reaching the dialectic, it is necessary to first pass through the decentering of consciousness as the place and origin of sense, then to cross an antithesis of interpretations, and finally to pass on to the dialectic.

The decentering of consciousness means that reflection is not intuition, that reflection is not immediate consciousness, and that it must become concrete. Ricœur elaborates this displacement or moving of the origin of meaning from consciousness in three directions. (CI, 23-27) The origin of meaning is rooted in desire, in the spirit and in the Sacred.

One type of interpretation has been placed in opposition to another so that one comes to light as progressive and the other as regressive. This shall also be discussed in considering the dialectic.

It is in further discussing the solution to the conflict between two opposed styles of interpretation in the dialectic of archeology and teleology that the other two phases will come to light and be further elaborated. But before beginning this discussion one more point must be clear. When Ricœur speaks of a dialectic he does not mean simply a dialectic between the archeology and the teleology as such. The dialectic is such that one interpretation is contained in the other, so that one comes to pass in the other, thus overcoming the antithesis. "Only at this moment is reflection truly in the archeology and the archeology in the teleology: reflection, teleology, archeology pass into one another. (DI, 477) This is the all-important point.

However, for Ricœur this dialectic is only the principle of the solution of the conflict. It is necessary to go beneath this dialectic to the concrete mixture giving rise to different interpretations each containing the archeology and teleology. This concrete mixture is the concrete symbol. (DI, 466) In order to understand more fully the dialectic in the concrete symbol we will begin with some remarks concerning the dialectic within interpretations.

Dialectic

Our concern with this dialectic worked out by Ricœur in the third book of *De l'interprétation* is with the *telos* and the *arché* of the teleology and archeology. We wish to bring to light the movement from their dialectical relation in the antithetical modes of interpretation to their dialectical relation in the texture of concrete symbols which gives rise to the different possibilities of interpretation. This movement will lead to the most ultimate *telos* and *arché* in eschatology. But at the same time it will throw light on the reasons for turning to concrete symbols in the midst of reflective philosophy and thereby carry on the discussion on the structure of the symbol. For it is from this analysis of the texture and possibilities of the concrete symbol that insight into the turn to concrete reflection as interpretation of symbols can be obtained.

Archeology of the subject

In discussing psychoanalysis in terms of an archeology of the subject and reflection, desire emerges as the *arché* and as the place of dependence of the *Cogito*. The problem revolves around desire and its relation to representation. The problem centers around what is presented in the affect but does not pass over into the representation. "That which is presented in the affect and which does not pass into the representation is desire as desire." (DI, 439) This indicates that the unconscious functionally is not language but pushes toward language. The regressive march toward desire as the limit which the unconscious imposes on linguistic transcription seeking it designates the *"sum"* of the *Cogito*. Thus Ricœur considers this function of desire to be at the origin of language and before language. (DI, 439)

Ricœur does not consider this problem as new to philosophy. "The question is common to all those philosophies which have tried to articulate the modes of knowledge on the modes of desire and of effort." (DI, 439) Although this is not a problem limited to Freud but has reference to the tradition of rational philosophy, the Freudian paradox contains a definite originality. The specific uniqueness of the Freudian paradox in viewing the bond between desire and representation, between effort and idea, is that the grasp by reflection of this bond is not possible by a direct grasping of consciousness; "the pre-reflective is powerless to reflect." (DI, 441) It is the psychoanalytic technique, the detour by another person, by the work, which serves for Freud as the intermediary. But Ricœur sees this not at all as suppressing the structural continuity between the unconscious and the conscious and the impulse-presentation and the representation. Rather, the affect of impulse-presentation has the function of presenting the body into the soul in the sense that in spite of the fact that desire is not nameable . . . "it is originally turned toward language; it wishes to be said; it is in the power of the word; that the desire be at the same time the non-said and the wishing-to-say (*vouloir-dire*), the unnameable and the power to speak, makes it the limit concept at the border of the organic and of the psychic." (DI, 441-442)

Law of double expressivity

The crux of Ricœur's analysis of this archeology of the subject is expressed in terms of the status of the representation in a concrete anthropology. (DI, 442) He wishes to place this status under the "laws of the double expressivity." The first is the law of intentionality which makes it the expression of something. The other law makes it the manifestation of life, of an effort or of a desire. It is the interference of this second expressive function which makes possible the distortion of the representation.

This double expressivity allows for a double investigation of the representation. The first considers the representation as an intentional relation ruled by the something which is manifested, and as such is what Ricœur calls a gnoseology. The other investigation is that of an exegesis of desire which is hidden. Each of these requires a sort of reduction by which the other is excluded. Thus the knowledge of the first type of investigation of the representation is abstract; and the reduction of knowing as such brings out the non-autonomy of knowing, its rootedness in existence understood as desire and as effort.

In that way is discovered not only the indepassable character of life, but the interference of desire with the intentionality on which it inflicts an invincible obscurity, an unrefusable partiality. By that finally is confirmed the character of the task of truth: the truth remains an idea, an infinite idea, for a being which first is born as desire and effort, or, to speak as Freud, as invincibly narcissistic libido. (DI, 442-443)

Teleology of the subject

Just as the above discussion on the archeology of the subject reveals the dependence of the *Cogito* on desire, a comparable discussion on the teleology of the subject brings to light a similar decentering of consciousness. This decentering or dispossession of consciousness is the spirit as a displacement of the *origin of sense,* not behind the subject, but in front of it. Ricœur does not consider this movement to a discussion on teleology of the subject simply a random movement, but rather one which is necessary from the nature of the subject with an *arché* reached in an analysis of archeology. The archeology of the subject remains abstract if it is not connected with its complementary term, teleology. "Only a subject which has a *telos* has an arché." (DI, 444) Thus again self-consciousness must be mediated.

> The subject . . . is never what one thinks it is. But it does not suffice for it to accede to its true being, that is discover the inadequation of the consciousness which it takes of itself, nor even the power of the desire which posits it in existence. It is still necessary that it discover that the 'becoming conscious' by which it appropriates the sense of its existence as desire and as effort, does not belong to it, but belongs to the *sense* which is made in it. It is necessary for it to mediate the consciousness of self by the spirit, that is, by the figures which give a *telos* to this 'becoming conscious.' (DI, 444).

It is in the connection between the archeology and the teleology of the subject that Ricœur hopes to come to the basis for the different modes of interpretation. And this connection is approached in the philosophy of the subject which comes to grips with the dialectic of the archeology and the teleology. However, the connection demands the investigation of teleology in Hegelian phenomenology of spirit, the implicit archeology contained in it, and the implicit teleology in Freudian analysis.

Ricœur takes up the discussion on Hegel's phenomenology as the model of every teleology of consciousness. He sees the same problem presented here as in Freud but in an inverse order. (DI, 446) Between the two, however, since they both deal with totalities, there can be only a relation of *homology*. (DI, 446) Whereas the order of movement in Freud is basically regressive in an archeology of the subject, it implicitly contains the teleology; and whereas Hegel's phenomenology is teleological, it contains implicitly and in a non-thematised way an archeology. If it were not for these non-thematised aspects, only an antithesis would be possible between the two. (DI, 452)

In taking Hegelian phenomenology as the teleological model of consciousness, spirit is understood as "a description of figures, of categories or of symbols which guide that crossing according to the order of a progressive synthesis," (DI, 447) Consciousness again does not move to self-consciousness except in becoming decentered and interpreted through the mediation of the movement of the spirit. Ricœur speaks of two guiding or directing themes which characterize a phenomenology of the spirit: the first concerns the synthetic, progressive movement which is contrasted to the analytical, regressive movement of the analysis of Freud. "In Hegelian phenomenology each figure receives its sense from the one which follows . . ." (DI, 448) The first guiding theme leads to the second: that which is in question in this movement is the production of the self of self-consciousness. The first theme is the key to the second because "the position of the self is in effect inseparable from its production by the progressive synthesis." (DI, 449)

From this consideration it is not difficult for Ricœur to move to the implicit archeology contained in Hegel's teleology. It is the role of desire in the movement to self-consciousness which brings to the fore the place of contact between Hegel and Freud, for it is in desire that the self prefigures itself and draws itself to itself; it is in the movement of desire that a culture is born. (DI, 449) They both agree also on the movement away from the object and toward the desire of desire. And it is the insurmountability of life and desire in the movement toward self-consciousness which allows the implicit *arché* to be made explicit in Hegel.

On the other hand, a non-thematised teleology can be drawn out of Freud without too much difficulty. Ricœur goes into a lengthy exposition on the various manners in which the non-thematised teleology can be extrapolated from Freud. It will be sufficient here for our purpose to repeat his brief outline at the beginning of his treatment and mention a few further remarks. (DI, 457)

What Ricœur is basically doing in this analysis and extrapolation is to find a basic finality in Freud. This finality can be summarized in the unique task of becoming-conscious "which defines the finality even of analysis." (DI, 474-475) He quotes Freud to this effect: "There where the *Id* was, the I should become." [33]

Ricœur sees this implicit teleology as discernible from the convergence of three types of indications: he sees first of all that certain operational concepts of Freudianism indicate it in non-thematised concepts, but which are at variance in the overall and dominating conceptuality of psychoanalysis. Such is the concept of identification. The third indication is in

[33] DI, 475: "Là où était Ça, doit advenir Je": quoting, "Wo es war, soll Ich werden."

the fact of some unresolved problems of psychoanalysis, such as sublimation, which are in the domain of psychoanalysis, but still not solved.

Thus we can see how Ricœur has attempted to work out the dialectic of
archeology and teleology in terms of the articulation of progression and
regression within each. In this manner he has brought reflection onto the
path to concrete reflection. Now he turns to the actual access to concrete
reflection itself. This is done in the realization that "progression and regression are carried by the same symbols, briefly, that the *symbolique* is
the place of the identity between progression and regression." (DI, 475)
This is the point toward which we have been working in this treatment of
the dialectic. For it is in this exposition that Ricœur brings to light the
access to the concrete by the symbol and thus allows us to come to the
central arguments for his turn to symbols and hermeneutics of them as
preliminary to a more explicit ontology.

Symbol as concrete mixture

We have already seen how Ricœur considers the dialectic of archeology
and teleology as the principle of a solution of the conflict in interpretations.
In order to reach the solution of the conflict it is necessary to go beneath
this dialectic to the concrete mixture giving rise to different interpretations.
This concrete mixture is the concrete symbol. (DI, 476) What he wants to
do now is to bring the dialectic down into the concrete symbol. In fact, for
Ricœur, "It is necessary to dialectise the symbol in order to think according to the symbol; only then it becomes possible to inscribe the dialectic in
the very interpretation and to make the return to the living word." (DI,
477) This marks the passage to concrete reflection. However, Ricœur is
careful to avoid a *naiveté* of immediacy. This is still reflection in the return
to the word as the intelligence of sense. It is a second naiveté; "it is post-
critical and not pre-critical." (DI, 478)

The ambiguity of the symbol, far from a weakness, is its strength in that
it allows for the working out of the dialectic by grounding it concretely.
Thus it is the same symbols which carry the two vectors: on the one hand
they are regressive, and on the other they are progressive. And it is not
simply a matter of being regressive or progressive in turn, but rather,
precisely by regressing to progress. It is precisely in the concrete structure
of the symbol that it unifies the revealing-hiding. At the same time that it
reveals it also hides. These are two sides of the unique symbolic function:
"at the same time that they hide the intentions of our impulses, they uncover the process of self-consciousness: to disguise, to unveil; to hide, to

reveal; these two functions are not any longer exterior to one another; they express the two faces of a unique symbolic function." (DI, 479) It is the symbol which by its surdetermination realizes the concrete identity between the progression of the figures of the spirit and the regression toward the signifying keys of the unconscious. "The forward movement of sense is pursued only in the milieu of the projections of the desire, of the rejections of the unconsciousness, the resurgence of the archaism." (DI, 479) Thus for Ricœur desire nourishes the symbols and symbols as images give figure to ideas.

Ricœur has returned to the central problem and theme of the section on the *arché* or archeology and the problem met there of the relation between representation and desire, or between effort and idea. There the first *arché* was seen to be desire. Thus the double expressivity allows for expression as manifesting desire and life besides the intentionality expressed. In the present context of the symbol it is the symbolic function which brings desire to the symbol thus serving as the ground for conflicting interpretations. And it is this symbolic function thus considered in which coincide the hiding – revealing, the disguising-unveiling. (DI, 479) And it is by the disguising, by the projection, that the uncovering and unveiling takes place, which subliminates human oneirism. (DI, 479)

The symbolic bond becomes problematical when the polysemy of the symbol is adverted to. For in discussing Freud's discourse on dream-interpretation, it is noticeable that the same things are always come to, the genital organs, the sexual relations and acts; but they are come to by any number of representations. "It is precisely the disproportion between the abundance of representations and the monotony of contents, . . . which poses directly the problem of the constitution of the symbolic bond." (DI, 481) The dream does not pose it because it presupposes it. In fact, we come to know the significations of the symbols of dreams from tales and myths, from folklore, etc. Thus it is, even as Freud himself admits, the work of culture which constructs the symbolic bond, which means that the bond is established in the language. Ricœur criticises Freud for reading this relation backwards, so that he tends to reduce the myth to the oneiric rather than see the myth first and then the possibility of the dream and its use of symbols from myth.

Ricœur considers Freud mistakenly to have limited the notion of symbol to usual, stenographic signs. Ricœur prefers to speak of the symbol as an aurora of sense. He proposes to distinguish several levels of creativity of the symbols. (DI, 486) First, at the lowest level there is the sedimented *symbolique*. This is the level of the stereotyped symbols which have only a past; the work of symbolization does not function there on that level. The *symbolique* of dreams has recourse to this level, as legends and tales.

Ricœur indicates the second level as comprising symbols with a usual function lacking to the first level to some extent. These are the symbols which are used with a past and a present. This is the level of structural anthropology since it serves as a gauge for the ensemble of social pacts within the synchrony of a given society. (DI, 486)

At a superior level are the prospective symbols which are "the creations of sense." As such, they take up again the traditional symbols with their available polysemy and carry new significations. "This *creation of sense* reflects the living basis not sedimented and not invested socially with symbolism." Ricœur will attempt to show later in this chapter that this creation of sense is at the same time a taking up again of the archaic fantasms and a living interpretation of fantasmic basis.

In looking at the dream from the perspective of this division or distinctions among symbolic levels, Ricœur places them as giving the key only to the first level, since Freud's use of symbols reveals only a falling back to the sedimented plain of sedimented expressions. What Ricœur would like to do is capture the symbol at the moment of its creation, in the level of creativity, rather than wait until it is sedimented and recurs in the dream. This we will see again later when he turns explicitly to the problem of the phantasm and the creation of the symbol from it.

The Hierarchical order of the symbol

The discussion which takes place after the above distinctions and before the return to Ricœur's original question concerning religion and symbols is an attempt to apply the regressive and the progressive aspects of the symbol to more particular problems. In the process the guideline followed is the one followed in order to articulate feeling. He wants here to put to the test the principle of hierarchy used in that context. He wishes here to focus on the problem of mixture taking it up now in the context of the antithesis of the two hermeneutics. (DI, 487) "These same feelings which we formally studied under the sign of *thumos* have to appear to us today as tributary to two exegeses, one in the sense of Freudian erotic, the other in the sense of a phenomenology of spirit." (DI, 487) To this effect, Ricœur proposes to take up again the same trilogy of feelings as in those of *avoir, pouvoir,* and *valoir.* He wishes to show in the present context the authentic triple quest as belonging to both a phenomenology of the spirit and to a Freudian erotic. (DI, 487)

What Ricœur proceeds at great length to do is to begin with the objec-

tivity which reveals the constitution of these feelings, or which is constitutive of them, and then afterwards, to go to their more libidinal constitution. So, since they are first constituted as non-libidinal spheres of signification, he begins with the Hegelian rendition and moves to the Freudian, which was lacking to his prior analysis in *L'homme faillible*. In the
latter treatment, he renders a libidinal interpretation of these three spheres.
The high point of each of these treatments is in the third realm of the
objectivity of culture, or the cultural objects. It is this realm especially
which constitutes the self in affective fragility. It is therefore on this level
and with regard to this third phase of the movement that Ricœur spends a
great deal of effort to dialectise the symbol using for this purpose the
symbols from *Oedipus Rex*. He attempts to base two different readings in
the same unity of the symbol and in its power to disguise and to reveal. (DI,
497) This allows him to proceed with his parallel analysis of the dialectic of
sublimation and of the cultural object which is somehow its noematic
correlate. He sees the tragedy of Sophocles as revealing more than the
antithesis and even more than the dialectic, but "binds in the same structure of the profound unity of disguise and of unveiling, bound in the same
structure of the symbol having become a cultural object." (DI, 499)

It is thus possible to put the oneiric and the poetic on the same symbolic
level or scale: the production of the dream and the creation of the work
of art are at two extremes on that level or scale, according to what predominates in the symbol: the disguise or distortion; or the unveiling or
revelation. (DI, 499) This brings out the functional unity between the
dreams and the creation and at the same time allows for the difference in
value which separates the dream from the more durable works capable of
becoming permanently part of our culture. The functional unity is due to
a functional continuity between the revealing and veiling or hiding which
takes place in both the dream and the creation, but in an inverse proportion.
(DI, 499)

The unity between the two, the dream and the creation, is due to the
fact that they both spring from the same hyletic, "from a same matter of
desire, which assures them unity." (DI, 500) "It is in the intentional structure that the symbol envelops at the same time the unity of a hyletic and
the qualitative diversity of aims and of intentions, according to which predominates in it the concealment of its *hyle* or the unveiling of another
spiritual sense." (DI, 501) What the dream lacks is the mediation of work
which incarnates the fantasm into a material and communicates it to the
public.

Thus regression and progression are no longer simply in opposition to one another. Rather they designate two extreme limits on a unique level of symbolisation and not so much two opposed processes.

There is a similar structure on the side of the cultural object as noematic correlate which corresponds to the dialectical structure of sublimation. "Only the surdetermination of the symbols permit one to carry a true dialectic which renders justice at the same time to an economic of culture and to a phenomenology of spirit." (DI, 503) Ricœur therefore wishes to interpret the phenomenon of culture as the milieu in which is sedimented the sublimation with its double valence of disguising and of unfolding. It is by the surdetermination of the symbol that the work of culture is joined to the world of life; "it is well where the *id* was that the I becomes." (DI, 503)

Sacred as ultimate telos and arché

We have already seen how the *Cogito* is decentered in two manners; first, by nature or desire as *arché*; and second, by spirit as *telos*. We must now consider a third dependence of the *Cogito* which is an ultimate dependence, a dependence on the *arché* of all *arché* and the *telos* of all *telos*. This will ultimately become a discussion of the movement from the phenomenology of spirit and psychoanalysis to a phenomenology of religion.

Ricœur has to begin this analysis by pointing out that the Totally Other ceases to be Totally Other as other as soon as it addresses me. He takes the kerygma, the good news, to be precisely this. "But, by its manner of approaching, of coming, it announces itself as Totally-Other as the *arché* and as the *telos* which I can conceive reflectively." (DI, 505) But in thus becoming an event in the human word the Totally-Other can only be recognised in the movement of interpretation, and thus can be arrived at in the context of the dialectic between archeology and teleology. "It is as horizon of my archeology and as horizon of my teleology that creation and eschatology is announced." (DI, 505) Thus Ricœur considers this *arché* and this *telos* as the horizon of my roots and as the horizon of my intentions respectively. This is how he arrives at the ultimate *arché* and *telos*, at the root of roots and the supreme of the supreme. Thus the movement or extension can be followed in both directions, that of the transition from phenomenology of the spirit to the phenomenology of the sacred; and from the psychoanalysis of Freud to the sacred.

The transition to the phenomenology of the sacred is reached by an admission of the difficulty of absolute knowledge in the phenomenology of the spirit of Hegel. It is not sufficient to say that the Sacred becomes the

telos of the teleology. What checks the absolute knowledge of self-consciousness is *evil*. The symbols of evil resist being grasped by rational
knowledge. While it is true that symbols give rise to thought, the symbols
of evil show that there is always more in the myth and in the symbols than
in all our philosophy; (DI, 506), and that even philosophical interpretations of symbols will never become absolute knowledge. Thus the symbols of evil bring Ricœur back to a fundamental point indicated in the introduction to *L'homme faillible,* that the *symbolique* is insurmountable, . . .
"at the same time that it speaks to us of the check on our existence and
on our power to exist, they declare a check on the systems of thought which
would swallow the symbols in an absolute knowledge." (DI, 507) Also,
there is another side of these symbols of the sacred, those of reconciliation.
Ricœur brings out three formulas for indicating how the *symbolique* of evil
is also a *symbolique* of reconciliation, but cannot in any way be converted
into absolute knowledge.

The symbols of the sacred designate the impact in culture of a reality
which the movement of culture cannot contain. It serves as an attraction or
appeal to the whole succession of figures of culture, as a *telos*. "The sacred
is its eschatology; it is the horizon which reflection does not understand,
does not encompass." (DI, 508) It is by its reflection to the immanent
teleology of the succession of figures that the sacred concerns that philosophy of spirit or culture as its eschatology. (DI, 508)

In the same manner the phenomenology of the sacred with its symbols
of the sacred is related to psychoanalysis in the same function of horizon.
Thus it becomes the *arché* of every *arché*. We must reflect for a moment
how this is so for it is necessary for the problem of faith to demand
demystification in order not to fall back into the antithesis prior to the
dialectic which we have already worked through.

This need arises because of the tendency of the horizon to be converted
into an object. Therefore Ricœur sees the manner of treatment of illusion
by Freud, Marx and Nietzsche as on a second level. This tendency to
convert the horizon into object, or this process of objectivation, is a more
fundamental level of illusion and is a return to the illusion of reason the
way Kant saw it. For Ricœur this is at the same time the birth of metaphysics and of religion; "of metaphysic which makes God a supreme being;
of religion which treats the sacred as a new sphere of objects, of institutions, of powers from now on inscribed in the world of immanence, of
the objective spirit, on the side of objects, the institutions of the powers
of the economic sphere. We will say that a fourth sphere of objects is born,
at the interior of the human sphere of the spirit. There are now sacred

objects and not only the signs of the sacred; the sacred objects besides the world of culture." (DI, 509)

It is this objectivation of faith which brings faith into the sphere of illusion, and is thus subject of an hermeneutic of the reductive style. (DI, 509) Freudianism is one of these. This reductive hermeneutics today has to become a cultural phenomenon. It must demystify the idols to which this tendency to objectivation leads. "That is why it is always necessary to kill the idol in order for the symbol to live." (DI, 510) The symbol's richness is in its ambiguity. And it is this ambiguity which makes possible the different valencies giving rise to different interpretations. "The 'symbol gives rise to thought,' but it is also the birth of the idol; that is why the critique of the idol remains the condition of the conquest of the symbol." (DI, 521)

CHAPTER VI

PHILOSOPHICAL REFLECTION AS HERMENEUTICS

INTRODUCTION

So far Ricœur's pure reflection, basic theory of symbols, conflict of interpretation, and hermeneutics have been presented. This chapter will have to explicate his deepening movement; therefore, the main purpose of this chapter is to show what the influences of Jean Nabert and Sigmund Freud have for Ricœur's view of reflection. Each of these in turn brought about an alteration in his reflective philosophy, both in relation to his movement to concrete reflection, as well as in his view of pure reflection. (CI, 260) We must see first how Nabert changed his view of reflective philosophy and then how Freud deepened this changed view.

Thus these next chapters will attempt to bring to the fore the changes and extensions which the philosophy of Ricœur has undergone. In this way we are fulfilling the plan outlined in chapter one; to show how and to what extent his philosophy has undergone both development and change, and that, in spite of the changes, the development has been to some extent consistent and continuous, and the hermeneutics of the later period has been presupposed by pure reflection, as well as, to a limited extent, has been anticipated by it.

REPRESENTATION AND THE LIMITS OF A PHENOMENOLOGY
OF THE WILL

What Ricœur has learned in his encounter with Nabert and Freud has profoundly affected and deepened the role of representation in his philosophy of the will.

Such is the ultimate root of our problem: it lies in this primitive connection between effort and representation, between the act of existing and the *signs* which we display through our deeds. Reflection must become interpretation because I can not grasp this act of existing anywhere else than in the signs scattered in the world.[1]

[1] Paul Ricœur, *Third Terry Lecture*, p. 13.

This insight is what has prompted him to return to the link between deeds and signs, "since the reflection on my deeds is an interpretation of my motives as signs of my intention." [2] Thus it will become clearer why "it is the status of the representation in reflective method which raises the question." (CI, 212 & DI, 442)

Ricœur has been heavily influenced by Nabert and Freud. He states explicitly that it is Nabert who first posed the question of the subject for him, and only after that did he confront Freud. Nabert has made Ricœur see the further importance of motivation in relation to acts in a dimension not clear to him at the first stage of his philosophy of the will. He later learned from Freud the further need to deepen his view of motivation relevant to the unconscious. To make clear the precise influences each of these had on Ricœur's later development, some summary points of influence will be presented before entering on an explicit discussion of the role and status of representation in reflection and interpretation.

NABERT'S INFLUENCE

Jean Nabert is the one who first made Ricœur aware that reflection must be interpretation. (CI, 169) This marks the first radical deepening in Ricœur's view of reflection. What Ricœur learned from Nabert is precisely this: first, it is from Nabert that he confronts the terse formulation of the relation between desire and effort and the signs in which these are expressed; second, it was from Nabert that Ricœur came to realize that to understand is inseparable from understanding oneself, i.e., "signs are . . . the milieu, the medium, thanks to which a human existent seeks to situate himself, to project himself, to understand himself"; (CI, 169) third, that reflection is not intuition, that there is no direct intuition of the self by the self. Reflection must become the interpretation of signs; the *Cogito* must be mediated by the whole universe of signs. Thus Ricœur is explicit in stating that it is not from the reading of Freud but from Nabert that he comes to his working hypothesis: "That working hypothesis, I do not conceal it, does not proceed from the reading of Freud; the reading of Freud meets it only problematically; it (the reading of Freud) meets it exactly in the point where, for Freud, it is also the question of the subject." (CI, 169-170)

FREUD'S INFLUENCE

After learning that reflection is interpretation and not intuition, Ricœur

[2] Paul Ricœur, *Third Terry Lecture,* p. 11.

learned from Freud the need to go beyond consciousness. He learned from Freud first, that consciousness is not the total source of meaning, and therefore must be decentered; "The sense of what I am is not given, but hidden; it can even remain indefinitely problematical, as a question without response." (CI, 238) In the words which Ricœur likes to use in a paraphrase of the Scriptures; "It is necessary to lose consciousness in order to find the subject." (CI, 239) Second: This point is a sort of reverse of the first. Becoming conscious is a task and not a given. This is a task of disillusionment, a movement from false or pseudo-consciousness to a deeper consciousness. "What Freud teaches us is that these notions of intention and motivation are not necessarily linked to that of consciousness, that there can be meaning before there is an explicit ego." [3] Third: that the signs which express meaning can be first deceptive and illusory. This is why a hermeneutics of a different kind from the progressive, synthetic movement of the interpretation of the phenomenology of religion is needed, to raise suspicion, to disillusion, to tear up the idols as a negative stage toward truth.

The interrelation of these insights obtained from Nabert and Freud will become more clear in the following discussion which will deal with the question of the "status of the representation in reflective method." (CI, 212) Thus we attempt to follow Ricœur's progressive deepening of reflective method.

STATUS OF REPRESENTATION

Two aspects of the status of the representation should be at the forefront throughout this discussion. The first is the founded character of the representation (CI, 211); Ricœur has always been consistent to this from the beginning of his writings on the philosophy of the will although he has lately come to understand it differently. From the beginning he has wanted to make willing the founding act, getting away from the Kantian and Husserlian epistemological prejudice. Thus, the representation is not the first function, the better known. Rather, "it becomes a second function of effort and of desire. It is no longer that which makes us understand but that which it is necessary to understand." (CI, 211) Instead of going through the representation to understanding by means of it, it is on the contrary necessary to work toward an understanding of the representation. This involves a going back from the representation to its foundation, to

[3] Paul Ricœur, "Philosophy of Will and Action," p. 31.

the origin of meaning. It is the link between the representation and effort and desire.

The second aspect of the status of the representation to be kept in mind is the "law of the double expressivity" of representation. In this "law of the double expressivity" of representation is found the intentionality and the reference to a subject which Ricœur has constantly maintained, from the eidetic level to the level of concrete reflection. This law of the double expressivity of the representation plays a central role in Ricœur's hermeneutics. For this law of representation is at the origin of the conflict of interpretation because it allows the concrete symbol to give rise to different interpretations, directed on the one hand ahead as a progressive interpretation, and on the other hand, directed backward as a regressive interpretation – with both capable of being articulated together in a dialectic and unified movement, as we have seen.

Ricœur attributes to Nabert his basic reorientation concerning this relationship between signs, representations, and acts. He is in agreement with Nabert's fundamental contention that it is necessary to read the relation between act, sign, and representation properly. (CI, 214)

What Ricœur has become aware of from Nabert is the relation of the motive to the representation and to the act. Since the representation is founded on willing, it is not the first function. To take it as such is misleading in giving us the meaning of existence. The motive comes to the representation and is prolonged in that way. But it is the sign of the meaning of the act. (CI, 215-216) As such it is the expression of the "unachieved act" or "unaccomplished act." But motives and values both can be read in two ways so that they can be seen as causes in the scientific psychological sense and as the sense of acts on the other hand. Thus it is possible in the first reading to "forget the initiative." Ricœur considers the earlier work of Nabert to be in the direction of a general theory of signs especially in its treatment of motives and value. In his later work, he goes beyond the epistemological question of the different centers of reflection to a more radical problem, that of existence and the existential duality. (CI, 218-219)

What Ricœur has learned from Nabert is precisely this: the link between deeds which reflect our effort and the notion of sign needing interpretation. (CI, 211-227) In his third *Terry Lecture* the link becomes the link between reflection and interpretation which is worked out with the concrete examples of decision. This link is what goes beyond the method of *Le volontaire et l'involontaire* or sees what it implies. For now Ricœur understands this reflection as interpretation, i.e., he understands a link between reflection and interpretation of the meaning of willing in the phase of deciding with motives. The question at hand is the relation between the two aspects of willing, the relation between intention and motivation. This is more or less the same question of *Le volontaire et l'involontaire*. But now, Ricœur sees the motive as the sign of the intention of willing. "There is no intuition of my power of will, of my effort and of my desire; I only grasp this power 'in' the *signs* presented (or represented) by my motives.[4] And Ricœur has learned from Freud that these signs are questionable, that they can be deceptive signs. There is therefore no definite, direct, and clear access to the meaning of my motives and therefore to the meaning of my intentions or acts. "The intention of my will can be read nowhere else than in these ambiguous signs of my power which I call the motives of my deeds." [5]

This is only one specific instance or dramatic aspect of the relation between willing and signs; between effort and its signs. "We may therefore generalize our remarks concerning the relation between the will and its signs and speak of a fundamental connection between the effort which constitutes our existence and the signs of this effort." [6] This is how reflection becomes interpretation; because these signs at the level of representation, which is founded on effort or desire or willing, must be interpreted.

Thus the central role of signs and representations emerges more clearly in the philosophy of Ricœur. However, great care must be taken in pointing out that this central role by no means is meant to make representation or sign founding instead of founded. But it is clear that because of this importance of signs or a theory of signs, Ricœur has considered it necessary to come to grips with the sciences which deal with sign. "This is why reflective philosophy has to include the results, the methods, the presuppositions of all the sciences which try to decipher and to interpret the signs of man." The reason is that the act of existing can be grasped only through signs scattered in the world.[7] Ricœur continually states the need to turn to these sciences.[8]

This line of development brings this consideration of reflection as interpretation to the threshold of the fundamental question of this treatise, concerning the implicit hermeneutic of the eidetic state. For it is clear that

[4] Paul Ricœur, *Third Terry Lecture*, p. 9.
[5] *Ibid.*
[6] *Ibid.*, p. 10.
[7] *Ibid.*, p. 11.
[8] Ricœur is constantly restating this: DI, 54; CI, 325; The *Third Terry Lecture*, p. 11.

any understanding or reflection on structures of willing must depend on interpretation of signs and is therefore hermeneutical. Not only that, since effort and desire are the two faces of the position of the self in the first truth "I am," [9] the interpretation of the signs of effort and desire is implicitly an interpretation of the "I am" and therefore enters the mainstream of problems concerning the question of the subject. This question is what is at stake in Ricœur's meeting the challenge of semiology. And, also, he wishes to approach the "I am" by a long way, gradually, instead of immediately entering upon a general hermeneutics of the "I am."

This also makes it clear why reflection is interpretation. For, to comprehend the act of existing, the effort to exist and desire to be must be reached and these are accessible only through signs. And the source of meaning is not first *je pense,* but it is rooted in desire. Ricœur finds it necessary therefore to turn to signs which express the meaning of our acts and symbols as access to the meaning of desire and the involuntary. He says this even as early as his essay "L'acte et le signe selon Jean Nabert," (CI, 211-222) and "Herméneutique et Réflexion." (CI, 311-329) "By this double access to value, the objectivation of the pure act and the symbolization of natural desire, we reach the center which is so much sought: as with Kant, 'the imagination makes the passage.' " (CI, 220)

EXTENDED VIEW OF REFLECTION

Ricœur's consideration of the nature of philosophy as reflection has been greatly altered. He has come to see all reflection on the self as interpretation. This view of reflection will be further elaborated in order to manifest the importance of signs in reflection and therefore in interpretation.

Following the vast tradition of modern philosophy from Descartes, Ricœur sees philosophy as reflection which focus on the self. After throwing all things, all external reality, into the darkness of doubt, Descartes was left with the self, with consciousness. For Descartes, the *Cogito* included the vast realm or realms of consciousness, and was given with any act. The *Cogito* and the *sum* are for the most part the same. That is to say, the self is intuited. There is an immediacy which seems to be quite apparent.

Ricœur discusses the position of the self for this whole modern tradition.[10] This whole tradition sees the position of the self as a truth which posits itself. "It cannot be verified, nor deduced; it is at the same time the

[9] Paul Ricœur, *Third Terry Lecture,* p. 7.
[10] Paul Ricœur, DI, pp. 59-61; CI, pp. 321-325; *Third Terry Lecture,* pp. 3-11.

position of a being and of an act; the position of an existence and of an operation of thought; I am, I think; to exist, for me, is to think"; (DI, 50) Since Descartes is speaking of a thinking substance when he says *"Cogito,"* it becomes clear that he is speaking of an intuition of oneself, so the *Cogito* and the *sum* are not too far removed from one another. This consciousness cannot be verified as a fact, nor can it be deduced as a conclusion, is neither empirical nor deductive, so it ought to posit itself in reflection. This means that the self in reflection is an immediate datum to this consciousness. This first truth is given in the evidence of immediate consciousness and remains "as abstract and empty as it is invincible." [11]

Ricœur moves now from the first reference of reflection to the positing of the self, as existing and thinking, to a second trait of reflection to become concrete, to encompass more than an abstract, empty self.

This second trait of reflection is that reflection is not intuition. (DI, 51) Here we see Ricœur departing from Descartes in favor of Kant. This means that the self, or the ego of the *Cogito* is not given immediately, not given as an object of intuition, nor in an intellectual intuition, nor in some kind of immediate vision. (DI, 51) "The first truth – I am, I think – has to be 'mediated' through the representations, the works, the deeds, the institutions, the monuments which objectivize it"; It is in these objects that the ego must find itself, since it has first lost itself in them, has first objectivized itself in them.[12] This can clearly be seen to mean that philosophical reflection can no longer be considered a philosophy of consciousness, if by consciousness is understood the immediate consciousness of self.[13]

Consciousness of the self now becomes a task since it is not given. It is true to say with Descartes that I do have an awareness of myself in acting, in thinking, etc. But Kant has sufficiently expressed this by stating that an apperception of the ego may accompany all my representations; but even for Kant, in order for this to be the case, an object or a representation is necessary in consciousness. Such an awareness, Kant has shown, is not knowledge, since it is not intuited. In fact, it is presupposed for knowledge as the other pole in the subject somehow related to the unifying categories. However, if we leave reflection on this level, it is strictly abstract. We have seen that reflection is not intuition, not meaning to leave the self completely out of the realm of knowledge, but rather to indicate another path for reflection. That path is the path of mediation. The self or the *ego* of the

---

[11] Paul Ricœur, *Third Terry Lecture*, p. 4.
[12] Paul Ricœur, DI, p. 51; *Third Terry Lecture*, p. 4.
[13] *Ibid.*

Cogito must be mediated for consciousness. And this brings us to the third characteristic or trait of reflective philosophy for Ricœur.

The third trait is a positive rendition of the second: that reflection is not intuition.

Reflection is not intuition. In positive terms, "reflection is the effort to regrasp the *ego* of the *ego cogito* in the mirror of its objects, of its works and finally of its acts." (DI, 51) In other words of Ricœur:

> Reflection is the appropriation of our effort to exist and of our desire to be, across the works which witness to this effort and this desire: This is why reflection is more than simply critique of knowledge and even more than a simple critique of moral judgement; before any critique of judgement it reflects on that act of existing which we unfold in effort and desire.14

The positive element introduced here is reflection as appropriation. And this appropriation is defended against Kantian limitation of reflection to epistemology, and against limitation to a strictly moral philosophy as a critique of moral judgement. Appropriation is of existence "which we unfold in effort and desire." This discussion must now turn to these expressions.

What does Ricœur mean when he says that reflection is appropriation or even reappropriation? Here he is getting back to the basic meaning of the French *propre* and one understanding of the English "proper." The basic meaning he intends is that which is "mine," "my own." This would mean in this context that we have to appropriate in the sense of making my own or of recovering what has been forgotten. I must render "mine" what has ceased to be "mine," what has first been lost. I am first lost among the objects and from the center of my existence. What has therefore to be recovered is the position of the self in its deeds, works and acts. The effort of existing has to be recaptured. This means then that the self does not possess first what it is. This is why consciousness, and therefore reflection must become a task, the task of "equating my concrete experience with the position: I am." 15 This insight springs from the founding character of the willing and the founded character of representation and knowledge.

At this point Ricœur again takes up the defense for the expansion of reflection beyond the limits of Kantian epistemology, and at the same time comes to grips with the objection against such an expansion as a limitation to ethics.

In this third trait of reflection as reappropriation, Ricœur disaligns him-

14 Paul Ricœur, DI, p. 54; *Third Terry Lecture,* p. 7.
15 Paul Ricœur, DI, p. 53; *Third Terry Lecture,* p. 56.

self from Kant by distinguishing reflection from a Kantian limitation to a mere critique of knowledge. Reflection for Kant is exclusively epistemology; it is concerned only with the a priori conditions for the possibility of knowledge, which support the objectivity of our representations. Kant is only concerned with the a priori and transcendental aspects or elements of knowledge. "What is a priori and not merely empirical in knowledge?" That distinction is the key to the theory of objectivity. And Kant merely transposes this question in the second critique. "The objectivity of the maxims of the will relies on the distinction between the force of duty which is a priori and the empirical desires." It is against this Kantian limitation of reflection that Ricœur agrees with Fichte and Jean Nabert that reflection is reappropriation of our effort of existing and not merely a justification of science and duty. Epistemology is only one part of a broader task, that of recapturing the act of existing.[16]

Ricœur's defense of this reflective philosophy against the objection that it is a limitation to ethics similar to the Kantian epistemology proceeds by showing how ethics has to be extended to a broader meaning. The end of this ethics is to seize the *ego* in its effort to exist and in its desire to be. Philosophy is then ethics since it leads from alienation to liberty and to happiness, to appropriation of the self, to self-consciousness. "That effort is a desire, because it is the affirmative position of a singular to-be and not simply a lack of to-be. Effort and desire are the two faces of the position of self in the first truth: *Je suis*." [17]

We stated above that Ricœur wants to root all reflection in life. In this third trait he has rooted it in the act of existing. But the act of existing must be read from the signs which we use in our works, deeds and acts. Reflection must not only become concrete, but must also become interpretation. Reflection must now for Ricœur dip down into the very concrete acts by which we project our existence, and read from these acts, works, deeds, through their signs, deeper meaning on the concrete, living, existing level. In this manner, Ricœur can be seen to come closer to the later Husserl when he roots signs in the perceptual and preperceptual levels and thus makes language a central question.

REFLECTION AND THE ORIGIN OF MEANING

Husserl's discussion of signs on the level of *Ursprung,* as preperceptual, has given language a central role in phenomenology. In turning to per-

[16] Paul Ricœur, DI, p. 54; *Third Terry Lecture,* p. 7.
[17] Paul Ricœur, DI, pp. 52-54; *Third Terry Lecture,* p. 7.

ception and to the preperceptual and pre-reflection as sign it is no longer the logical level of meaning alone, with the transcendental ego, but the total question of meaning which is considered.[18] In the *Logical Investigations* Husserl rooted the linguistic expression in the intentionality of consciousness in general, in lived experience. The manifesting function opened it to the subject and subjective experiences. This also holds true on the level of perception. Now these directions are lowered and made to apply to the whole question of meaning.

In considering the origin of meaning, the opening of the sign system is rendered more thematic. For the origin is behind and before consciousness, and ultimately, beyond consciousness. The further question is how the meaning comes to the sign. The origin of meaning is based on three decenterings of consciousness as we have already seen. Ricœur is constantly referring to this point in his recent writings.[19] These decenterings are: spirit, desire and the Sacred. The point of articulation, the point of crossing of these three is the symbol. And on each is based a type of hermeneutic. The question which is at issue is how they come to the representation. What relation is there between this pre-reflective signification and the representation. Ricœur deals with this question in the *De L'interprétation* and in articles in *Le Conflit des Interprétations*.[20] It is only here that we can return to the relation between this rooting of signs at the deepest level, and its influence on the perceptual field, on action and on living. At any rate, the deepening of the level of meaning is at the same time a deepening of the *Cogito,* or of the subject who "is the one who lives across the intentions of sense and is constituted as the identical pole of all the levels of sense." (CI, 243)

In this context Ricœur has spoken of a late grafting of hermeneutics onto phenomenology at the levels of signification and of the *Cogito*. (CI, 20-21) It is at these deepened points, the sign and its subject, below perception. The grafting for Ricœur takes place in the Husserlian context of the question of the totality of meaning. This also brings up the three central points of phenomenology for Ricœur: reduction, signification, and the subject: reduction as the means of access to meaning or signification; meaning as traversed by intentions of the subject.

---

[18] Paul Ricœur, "Husserl and Wittgenstein," in *Phenomenology and Existentialism,* p. 208.
[19] Paul Ricœur, CI, *passim;* DI, *passim.*
[20] We have considered this relation to some extent in the last chapter.

REFLECTION, SIGNS AND LANGUAGE

We have so far followed Ricœur in the extensions of all reflective philosophy and seen that all reflective philosophy is hermeneutical, and even eventually required a hermeneutics of suspicion. Furthermore, we have come to realize the need to turn to signs and their meaning in order to arrive at or appropriate the meaning of the self. This need of an indirect access to the meaning of the self mediated through signs has made the whole of semiology or the sciences of signs emerge, including psychoanalysis as well as the sciences of language. The detour into a depth study of Freudian psychoanalysis has already been presented. It remains for us to settle some of the difficulties and ambiguities in Ricœur's detours to the sciences of language as semiology and to see what further influences these semiological sciences will have on his later positions. For this encounter with the sciences and other studies of language has certainly not left him unaffected.

However, before embarking on such an undertaking, it will be helpful for the sake of the continuity and clarity of our development to fill in the gap between such a study of language and the present context of reflection. Therefore, the main contours, polarities and tensions of Ricœur's language theory shall be presented, but in the overall context of its relation to reflection. This will help us to tie up the movement of the last two chapters with the next chapter (VII).

LIMITS OF LANGUAGE

Ricœur's phenomenology of language has certain limits and goals or directions which he explicitly states. For Ricœur, as for Dufrenne,[21] phenomenology of language is only on the way to ontological language, the meeting place of his theory of language with Heidegger's. His problems later become different as he explicitly points out. (CI, 96) Nevertheless this ontology of language is the direction in which he is going as his horizon. "But if that ontology of language cannot become our theme, by reason of the procedure of this study, at least it can be viewed as the horizon of this research. Considered starting from this horizon, our investigation seems moved and guided by a conviction, that is, that the essence of language begins beyond the closure of signs." (CI, 96) The manner in which Ricœur makes this the horizon of his whole theory of language, and

---

[21] Mikel Dufrenne, *Language and Philosophy,* trans. by Henry Veatch, *passim.*

indeed of his theory of signs in general, will become clear. Actually, he began with his theory of symbols close to Heidegger's ontology of language and was working closer to that horizon than he does in many of the later articles in which he comes to grips with the theories of linguistics and correlative sciences of language. Throughout all treatments of problems of language and hermeneutics, this ontology of language and a general hermeneutics is clearly the goal and the force guiding the development. In considering other problems which Ricœur has had to face, it will become explicitly clear to what extent and how his consideration of language is different from Heidegger's. But, let it be said again, and in his own words, ontology is his horizon: "Thus, ontology is indeed the promised land for a philosophy which begins with language, and with reflection; but, as Moses, the speaking and reflecting subject sees it only before dying." (CI, 28) In other words, ontological language arises only at the end of the road, and after some decentering passage.

Tension and polarities within language

This tension between extremes can be seen when we consider the overall range of expressions giving rise to different levels or types of language. If we focus on the logical level of meaning and of the language which expresses it, we are on the level of Husserl's *First Investigation,* and on the level especially of empty signification. This would be, for instance, the empty language of abstract, symbolic logic. We can see the other extreme at the level of the concrete, full language of experience, especially the mythical language of experience and the concrete language of symbols.

The reason it is necessary to turn to language at this point is that the logical level as the *telos* of consciousness has the logical level of meaning as the *kinds* of linguistic expressions.[22] In considering them as rooted in linguistic expressions, the question of language at least at its logical level becomes important. But this is not the only level of meaning expressed in linguistic expressions so that the meaning of linguistic expressions opens up language for further consideration, especially as the linguistic expressions are rooted in the intentions to mean, or the subjective lived experiences as meaning-giving acts. When intentionality becomes the basis of linguistic expressions, then consciousness in general as intentional is brought to the fore and not just the level of logical meaning. Thus the total question of meaning arises so that the other direction, that of the source

[22] Paul Ricœur, "Husserl and Wittgenstein," p. 208.

and origin, comes to the fore. And this is the level of consciousness in general and of the *Ursprung*.[23]

What Ricœur attempts to do is to move from this logical level of meaning to the level of the origin and source of all levels of meaning in the language of experience. He has worked back from the totally abstract view on the tension between the polarities of the human antinomy toward the concrete level of this antinomy and human unity but cannot grasp it by pure reflection. When he comes to the level of the original, the level of the *Ursprung,* he finds that he must turn to the expressions of this level in which this tension and polarity are expressed. What this means is that the direction or orientation of consciousness which can be seen at any level within the continuum is itself rooted in linguistic expressions. Consequently, no matter what level of expression we focus on, there is the direction toward both poles. This means that if we start at the level of the *telos* and logical level of meaning at the *telos* extreme, there is the reference back to the source and origin. And if we start at the level of the original as *Ursprung,* there is the orientation to the *telos* of rationality.

What this ultimately means is that, first of all, language itself is intermediary between the two basic orientations or polarities, between the *telos* of logicity and the *Ursprung* of experience. But these two poles, the *telos* and the *Ursprung,* both come to linguistic expression or try to come to linguistic expressions. Thus linguistic expressions can be approached from two directions: we can descend upon them from the direction of logical contents; and we can ascend to them from the basic level of lived experience as Ursprung. And even though there are other products, deeds, acts, or works of man in which he as a mixture is expressed, the most totally extensive is that of language. And it has many unique aspects which shall come to light as making it advantageous as a place of focusing.

We can investigate further this tension within language by beginning with the logical level. Husserl's *First Investigation* is primarily concerned with the logical level and its foundation in the subject which does not destroy its ideality. Ricœur has indicated that it is this level of logical structures which is the *telos* of all expressions. [24] But even on this level we must be able to see clearly and explicitly the orientation toward the origin, the tendency or at least the opening in the direction toward the *Ursprung.*

It is the logical meaning as the kind of certain expressions which is the aim of all other levels. Thus it is this *logos* of rationality to which all levels of meaning and consciousness tend. And this level as that toward which

[23] Paul Ricœur, "Husserl and Wittgenstein," p. 209.
[24] *Ibid.*, p. 208.

the others aim does not have to be fulfilled, does not need the presence of the object for Husserl. There is the possibility on this level of empty language such as symbolic logic. However, even at this highest level of the logical, consciousness is intentional in its act. In fact, we can speak of the empty expression precisely because this expression has a referring function which seeks fulfillment.

It is the focus on intentionality which gives rise to the direction or path to the *Ursprung*. For the focus on the subjective lived experience as acts of intention is rooted in the basic intentional character of consciousness as consciousness of . . . and brings the discussion and search to bear on the source, the origin, and the genesis of meaning even of the objectivity and ideality of meaning of the type in the *First Investigation*. Thus we can see more clearly the tendency to the source even at this level of the *telos* or final level.

This level of the logical as *telos* is what Ricœur wishes not to forget. This is one reason for his criticism against the too quick movement to the *Lebenswelt*. He does not wish to loose the orientation of consciousness even on the level of its most original expression to the level of rationality.

We have seen how even at the highest level of the *telos* there is the possibility and tendency to go back to the origin, or at least, the path has been left open as a possibility. However there is some difficulty in trying to travel along this path. The difficulty arises from the fact that this level is not directly given, that the access to the *Ursprung* is a backward movement. It has been called a *Rückfrage*, a questioning back to the source.

There is a further difficulty in searching for or in trying to reach the level of *Ursprung*. This springs from overcoming the logistic prejudice toward the strictly theoretical and the movement to the practical and the affective. In this consideration of the *Ursprung*, especially as it comes to language, we must be clearly aware that it is not only the theoretical, but the practical and the affective which Ricœur wishes to see as coming to language. The language toward which he has worked back in his *Rückfrage* is that of experience, and especially the language of symbolic expressions.

Ricœur attempts to root all philosophy and thinking in life as *Ursprung*. He considers the basic quest of man synthesizing the *Logos* and *Bios* in three moments, that of the *avoir*, that of the *pouvoir* and that of the *valoir*, as has been already mentioned in chapter three. He proceeds by considering the correlate objectivities which these intend and which leads to the language of cultural expressions as expressions of this level with its basic orientations and polarities. And the unity of intentionality and affection allows for the movement from the objectivity to the self affected and allows this from the beginning in the language of myths and of symbols.

What comes to light in this manner of investigation is the twofold or double intentionality of these expressions, which is so illuminating for Ricœur's study since it allows for an indirect access to the basic intentionality of consciousness.

And thus the further problem emerges in considering this access. In attempting to explicate this level of the *Ursprung* by the use of hermeneutics of symbolic expressions which reveal the double intentionality and thus express life, we find a conflict of interpretations. And it is in working out this conflict that different aspects of intentionality come to light, revealing the nature of man's bond or link to the world and to being. The same symbols allow for different and conflicting readings and interpretations. On the one hand, they can be interpreted by the phenomenology of religion, and on the other hand, they can be interpreted in an opposed way in the psychoanalytical manner.[25] This is the problem in the access to the fundamental level of origin. It seems to augment the objections to seeking access to the level of experience through language of symbols. However, in the working out of the solution to this conflict in interpretations on the fundamental level, fuller insight and grasp of this level has been obtained. And in the solution to this conflict the advantage of the hermeneutics of symbols is indeed access to lived experience. In working out this conflict the link or bond that underlies the subject-object dichotomy comes to light, not simply as such but as a multi-dimensional bond or link, one which does not immediately reveal itself, and one which is not too quickly grasped in its unity. This is the attempt on the part of Ricœur to bring out further the constantly reaffirmed conviction that man, even on the level of the *Cogito* and willing, is receptive, that the voluntary and *Cogito* only constitute what it receives as origin. The extent of this receptivity will be further discussed in the concluding chapter.

Indirect access to Ursprung

It is clear by now that Ricœur is convinced of the indirect accessibility of the *Ursprung*. This is the case because the *Ursprung* as origin and as horizon is not given so that it is grasped by a questioning back, by a *Rückfrage*. As the horizon of particular acts of consciousness it is presupposed as their condition. However, the *Rückfrage* as a simple questioning back does not fully bring to light the *Ursprung* or origin. For him it is necessary

[25] We have considered this problem at length in chapter five.

for the *Rückfrage* to become hermeneutics which reveal the *Lebenswelt* level by means of the passage which they initiate from one sense to a second sense and a second intentionality. We have seen in chapter five how this reveals a threefold decentering of consciousness. The origin of meaning comes to light in different aspects of existence which the solution of the conflict in interpretations has shown us.

It is clear that a view of reflection hinges on a view of signs and especially a view of language signs. So far Ricœur's view of the nature of reflection has been considered from a point of view prior to his serious attempt to encounter the challenge of the semiological sciences of language. It would be a misrepresentation of his later development to stop with his encounters with Nabert and Freud. For his encounter with these theories of language has required considerable broadening, important for his view of reflection, hermeneutics and a philosophy of the will.

CHAPTER VII

PHENOMENOLOGY AND THE SCIENCES OF LANGUAGE: FURTHER EXTENSIONS

An ambiguity emerges from some of Ricœur's recent writings on language. On the one hand, he considers it necessary today for phenomenology of language to take the sciences of language seriously; on the other hand, in many of his writings on the sciences of language, he appears to dismiss them rather than take them seriously. In further investigating this ambiguity, we will come to see how he has further developed his philosophy of language, and how this is the point of several important extensions central to his later philosophy.

This ambiguity, arising from what Ricœur considers a necessary confrontation between semiology and phenomenology, can be further polarized. "The detour through the sciences of language is not something one can choose or not choose to make: it is essential to phenomenology today if it is to survive." [1] He seems to take the sciences of language so seriously that he considers semiology the entrance to phenomenology. Semantics and phenomenology have their basis and support in semiology. He even wants to enter semiology and make the passage to semantics from semiology. He seems to consider phenomenology radically challenged by the sciences of language. And for phenomenology to survive, it must confront the sciences of language in such a way as to answer this challenge, whatever it is.

Another side of the ambiguity raises the question of the seriousness of Ricœur's confrontation. If he really considers semiology to challenge phenomenology, then the confrontation should be a serious one. It must really spring from a radical challenge levied at the very roots and radical possibility of phenomenology. But instead, Ricœur seems at first merely to turn to semiology with the sole intention of destroying it, of pitting phenomenology of language against it, in order to revive phenomenology, which actually is not threatened and has not changed.

If Ricœur really considers semiology to challenge phenomenology, then

[1] Paul Ricœur, "New Developments in Phenomenology in France," p. 14.

he must consider semiology to have an element for which phenomenology must be able to account. This element must be so essential to the language phenomenon that it must come into any account of language today, after having come to the fore in these sciences. And this element or aspect is one for which phenomenology has not sufficiently accounted.

Thus the need for phenomenology to confront semiology and the sciences of language is not merely a factual or historical one arising from two conflicting contemporary views of language. Rather, each has a truth according to Ricœur, and each viewpoint must be able to render account of the truth or essential element of the other.

The plan of this chapter will therefore be, first, to highlight the nature of the challenge: then to oppose these two points of view: and to bring to light Ricœur's theory and view of language which demands, not an opposition, but an interarticulation. After such a consideration, the ambiguity to some extent disappears, when it becomes clear why Ricœur considers it necessary for the phenomenology of language to turn to semiology and how each perspective instructs the other.

NATURE OF THE CHALLENGE

If the detour through the sciences of language is necessary for phenomenology to survive, the challenge must threaten phenomenology at its center. And Ricœur considers it to do just that. The three essential elements of any phenomenology are reduction, signification and the subject. (CI, 242-243) And the semiological science leaves little room for these elements. The positive element or aspect of semiology excludes the possibility of phenomenology; it imposes such a condition that phenomenology cannot survive. The precise nature of this challenge must be further illuminated.

The real challenge from semiology arises from its fundamental principles and orientations toward the language phenomenon. The challenge which Ricœur indicates is precisely this: if linguistic science is left in its extreme, it leaves no room for phenomenology of language. If language is focused on as an empirical object, and signs are meaningless unities in relation to others in the whole system, the constitution of the sign (word) is such that a phenomenclogy of speech is completely excluded. Signification and a subject have little place in such a theory of language. "The challenge consists in this, that the notion of signification is placed in a field other than the intentional aim of a subject. The displacement is quite comparable to that which psychoanalysis imposes on the effects of sense of immediate consciousness. (CI, 246) The challenge then is the result of the semiological view. Thus, to grasp the depths of the challenge, it is necessary to make the detour to this science of signs. The extreme opposition between that science and phenomenology will thus come to light.

However, it is already clear that if there really is such an opposition, not only phenomenology but also semiology and linguistic science are radically challenged. If they are antinomical views dealing with the same phenomenon, the confrontation cannot result merely in a juxtaposing or an opposing of one to the other. If they are possible together, they must be interarticulated. And this is precisely what Ricœur has in mind. He is attempting to interarticulate these different attitudes, but not at the price of an eclecticism. And if he really takes seriously this challenge, if he really considers phenomenology to be radically challenged, his interarticulation must account adequately for some positive truth from the sciences of language. He must account for their validity and for their possibility.

Therefore, the sciences of language are likewise radically challenged by the phenomenology of language. The phenomenology of language also has a positive element or truth which the sciences of language must be able to account for, yet it cannot account for it without undergoing some change. Therefore, from this confrontation, both phenomenology and semiology must undergo some radical adjustment, if the opposition and contradictions between them are radical. From his extreme statement about the confrontation, it is clear that Ricœur sees how semiology excludes phenomenology, and yet, that phenomenology must learn from semiology in order to survive. "This reanimated phenomenology can not be content with repeating the old descriptions of speech which do not recognize the theoretical status of linguistics and its first axioms, the primacy of structure over process." [2] The condition imposed by semiology on phenomenology is such that it is "through and by means of a linguistic of language that a phenomenology of speech is today conceivable." [3]

Semiology places this condition on phenomenology: that phenomenology be able to account for a theory of structures, for the system or semiological model, i.e., for a theory of constitution and relation of signs. But phenomenology places a condition on semiology: that it adequately account for meaning; for that which is said in speaking.

The opposition between semiology and phenomenology will be further investigated before discussing Ricœur's attempt to interarticulate these approaches. He considers it necessary to see the antinomy in order to find the place of contact. However, in presenting the opposition, the mutual

[2] Paul Ricœur, "Philosophy of Language," p. 19.
[3] *Ibid.*

exclusiveness of the two approaches to language will be stressed, in order to highlight the need for some adjustment, both in phenomenology and in semiology. This will indicate more clearly the limitations of each method, at the same time as it clarifies the radical nature of this two-directional challenge.

OPPOSITION

By following Ricœur's own treatment of the opposition between semiological science and phenomenology, we will be able to see if he actually dismisses them in favor of his phenomenology or if he radically opposes them, in order to reach a serious interarticulation. It will then become clear to what extent he really takes the challenge seriously.

The five presuppositions of semiology which Ricœur confronts are as follows. The first distinguishes language (*le langage*) into scientific language (*la langue*) and speech (*la parole*). This distinction makes language (*la langue*) an object of empirical science, with its rules constituting the code and its aspects of institution and social restraint. Thus, "everything which concerns a language falls, in effect, within the same domain, while speech is dispersed among the registers of psychophysiology, psychology, sociology and does not seem to be able to constitute the unique object of a specific discipline." (CI, 82) This first presupposition is the most radically opposed to phenomenology, as we shall see. It to a large extent implicitly contains the others. Thus, most of this (Ricœur's) opposition and interarticulation can be considered to focus on this distinction of language into scientific or empirical object and speech.

The second presupposition of semiology entails a further distinction springing from the first. The place of this distinction is important, especially considering Merleau-Ponty. (We shall consider Merleau-Ponty's interpretation of these two presuppositions later.) This second presupposition is the relation of diachrony and synchrony. It not only distinguishes between a science of static states of a system or synchronic linguistics, and a science of change – diachronic linguistics: it subordinates diachrony to synchrony. Therefore, it subordinates history to system, change to structure. What changes will be understood from what does not change. Change is understood as the passage from one state of the system to another. As we shall see, this understanding of the distinction and relation between synchrony and diachrony differs from Merleau-Ponty's interpretation of Saussure.

The third presupposition states that language (*la langue*) is simply a system of signs, with only relations of mutual dependence. (CI, 246) This stresses form in language and not content or semantics. For Ricœur it means ". . . that we need not consider the meanings attached to isolated signs as labels in a heteroclite nomenclature, but only relative, negative values of signs with respect to each other." (CI, 82-83)

The fourth presupposition merely develops the third. According to it, the system of signs is a closed system ". . . an autonomous entity of internal dependencies," (CI, 81) and therefore can be an object of analysis.

These four presuppositions necessitate a fifth: that the definition of sign be changed so that a sign does not stand for a thing. Sign must be defined ". . . not only by its relation of opposition to all other signs of the same level, but also in itself as a purely internal or immanent difference." (CI, 83) This definition keeps to the closure of the universe of signs as a closed system, so that the sign is either a difference between signs or an internal difference between expression and content.

These presuppositions bring about a radical and serious opposition between phenomenology of any kind and the science of language. But Ricœur is very careful about how this opposition should be read. And he refuses to read it the way Merleau-Ponty does. He criticizes Merleau-Ponty's opposition for failing to come to grips with the problem. Ricœur is convinced that the manner in which Merleau-Ponty considers language pushes it into a central position in phenomenology, but in such a way that it excludes any "dialogue with modern linguistics and semiology established on a linguistic model." (CI, 244) By considering some points of Merleau-Ponty's phenomenology of language regarding the above presuppositions of semiology, Ricœur's different manner of opposing semiology and phenomenology becomes clear. This different opposition not only makes possible a dialogue with linguistics, but it makes such a confrontation necessary if phenomenology of language is to survive in an interarticulation.

The first emphasis of Merleau-Ponty is the turning to the speaking subject as distinct from the objective language, thus opposing phenomenology of language as a return to the speaking subject, to the objective, scientific attitude. Merleau-Ponty therefore wants to oppose and separate the two sides of language distinguished by Saussure and read the unity of language on the side of the speaking subject. He makes the science of language deal only with past language, and makes the system spring from the actuality of speech. Ricœur considers this an erroneous interpretation of Saussure. "Merleau-Ponty thinks he is in agreement with Saussure when he attributes to him the distinction between 'a synchronic linguistics of speech and a diachronic linguistics of language.' This is obviously an error." [4]

Actually, recalling the second presupposition, Saussure has distinguished diachrony and synchrony both on the side of *la langue*. And this is the way Ricœur wants to see it. Putting them together renders the problem of subordination more difficult and more crucial.

Consequently, Ricœur accuses Merleau-Ponty of not allowing any place for the sciences of language (CI, 244) and of not taking linguistic science seriously. The weakness of the phenomenology of language (of Merleau-Ponty) is its failure to consider language as an autonomous system, and its treatment of sedimentation in terms of psychological gesture and habit without coming to grips with the other structural elements of the system.

Already the opposition is becoming clear. But the further development of the opposition requires a critique of Merleau-Ponty, at the same time as a reopposing of phenomenology and linguistics. This makes clearer just how Ricœur sees the opposition. Several points of opposition must be considered: (1) *la langue* as object and speech; (2) the relation between diachrony and synchrony; and (3) the sign system as a closed, independent system, and the openness of signs.

1. *Object vs. Mediation*

The real root of opposition between phenomenology of language and semiology is the view of language as object, and the view of language as mediation. On the one hand, semiology does not allow for language as a mediation. It considers *la langue* as an empirical object. Semantics and phonology are not essential in the extreme statement of linguistics by Saussure. (Other linguists are not so extreme.) The semantic is derived from the semiological. The function or use of language is not determining. Rather, the scientific system, the empirical science of language is determining. The language object is independent of use and therefore isolated from a speaker or subject and from meaning. The opposition regarding this distinction is between a phenomenology which cannot give up the primordial importance of consciousness, of the subject, of meaning in language, and a linguistics which cannot give up the scientific aspect of language.

2. *Diachrony and Synchrony*

This second point of opposition is the relation between diachrony and synchrony. The opposition presented by the manner of reading this relation

[4] Paul Ricœur, "Philosophy of Language," p. 12.

arrives at the very heart of both phenomenology and semiology. If the relation is read the way in which Saussure reads it, so that diachrony is subordinated to synchrony, system predominates over change; this results in a stress on static language. Both diachrony and synchrony are on the side of *la langue*. Speech, the concern of phenomenology, has no scientific unity and cannot be considered by any one science.

The opposed view presented by a phenomenology of language is not for Ricœur that of Merleau-Ponty. Rather, the opposition is not between a synchronic speech and a diachronic past language. Ricœur wants to see the relation of subordination in a way opposed to linguistics. Thus, synchrony is subordinated to diachrony.

3. *Closed System of Signs and Openness*

The third point of opposition is presented by the view of the closed system of signs, opposed to the openness of signs. The linguist, as we have seen, considers *la langue* to be constituted by a closed system of signs. The signs are only relations of mutual interdependence. As such, signs are independent as is the whole system. Signs do not have a reference, they are cut off from the world. They are in no way bound to or by a reference intended or referred to something. Likewise, they do not manifest a subject. They are closed to the I who speaks.

The opposition to phenomenology is apparent. For the phenomenologist, linguistic expressions are meaningful signs with manifesting, meaning, and referring functions.[5] Signs have a meaning which refers. And signs manifest lived experience of a speaker. The closed system of signs is cut off, closed off from the world and from the I.

The manner in which Ricœur approaches this opposition can easily lead to a misinterpretation. He considers the limitations of the scientific linguistic approach and the need to go beyond semiology. But this does not necessarily lead to the conclusion that he does not take them seriously, or that he has not altered phenomenology. In this confrontation he is attempting to see how phenomenology must be adjusted in order to receive the truth of semiology. He expresses the problem well when he says: "My problem becomes more precise: what is the place of a 'general theory of relations' in a general theory of sense?" (CI, 42) But he begins by considering the failure or weakness of semiology. If he ends up by completely disregarding the fundamental insight and possibility of semiology and linguistic science, he has wasted a lot of time with his detour to semiology.

[5] Edmund Husserl, *Logische Untersuchungen* (3 vols.; Max Niemeyer Verlag: Tübingen, 1968), II, pp. 23-106.

INTERARTICULATION

In order to understand Ricœur's attempt to go beyond that opposition, it is necessary to realize that he does not agree with the initial distinction between *la langue* and *la parole*. He wishes rather to consider the unity of *le langage* fundamental to both and unifying them in a hierarchy of levels: "to think language (*le langage*) should be to think the unity of that very reality which Saussure has disjoined – the unity of language (*la langue*) and speech." (CI, 86) But to make this interarticulation which would do justice to a phenomenology of language coming to grips with semiology, the extremes of semiology must be overcome. Ricœur sees the need to mitigate the over-absolutization of linguistic science. By over-absolutizing the language object, linguistic science cannot account for meaning. Ricœur does not object to the constitution of language as an empirical object yielding science, if the scientist "keeps the critical consciousness that that object is entirely determined by the procedures, the methods, the presuppositions, and finally the structures of the theory which regulates its constitutions." (CI, 85) Such a critical attitude prevents making that phenomenon an absolute. Thus, the linguistic object must not be separated from its subordination to method and theory. If this is not kept in mind, the essence and goal of language is jeopardized by the scientist. For meaning is taken out of discourse. There is no longer room for saying something about something, for the free combination and selection necessary for poetic language.

New Unity of Language

In order to move from the opposition to interarticulation in language, Ricœur must move to a new unity, a unity which allows for the articulation of the sciences of language, and at the same time does not exclude the essence of language as the saying of something about something. This new unity allows for the science of language by articulating various levels of language together, with a break at one point in the hierarchy.

Ricœur looks for a new unity of language which will do justice to both semiology, which takes language as object, and to phenomenology of speech. But his intent is to get away from that distinction between language (*la langue*) and speech as a false dichotomy. Consequently, he looks for a unity which will allow for articulating both aspects of language together. This unity is needed if the opposition is to be surpassed. The new unity must at the same time allow for the possibility of viewing language abstracted from its use or function as an object of science and also allow for the communication event. It must serve as a ground for the distinction between *la langue* and *la parole*. However, this new unity will require certain radical alterations in semiology. Semiology will have to admit certain limitations: that, in order to render language an object of science the way in which semiology does, it is necessary to give up certain essential aspects of language; that semiology always presupposes certain functions and elements which it does not avert to or admit; that this function and aspect of language is common to all language, and therefore must be accounted for in the semiological system or at least made room for. "The consciousness of the validity of a method is never separable from the consciousness of its limits." (CI, 34)

The new unity of language reaches the crux of the confrontation. This unity for Ricœur is put on the side of semantics. What is at stake is the primordial role of semantics. The question then is whether semiology and syntax or semantics should yield the unity. And Ricœur definitely thinks the best unity is on the side of discourse, of function, of semantics. This is for several reasons: (1) Semantics and semantic function is presupposed by all sciences of language. For Ricœur all roads lead from semantics – in the sense that they presuppose it at least implicitly. (2) By putting the unity on the side of semantics, in the sentence, Ricœur sees that both sides of the antinomy or opposition can be articulated. We have already seen this opposition. In putting the unity in the sentence, an articulation of hierarchical levels of language is necessary. "In short, the linking of methods, of points of view, of models, is a consequence of the hierarchy of levels in the work of language." (CI, 81) It is, then, this hierarchy of levels which makes possible the interarticulation of the various approaches. But, "my whole study will rest on the idea that the passage to the new unity of discourse constituted by the sentence or enunciation represents a break, a change, in the hierarchy of levels." (CI, 81) And, to understand this hierarchy of levels with the break, it is necessary to consider the fundamental point at the center of Ricœur's reflection which demands this change of the unity of language (*le langage*).

The strength of Ricœur's position rests on the insight that the sciences of language presuppose a semantic function which they do not necessarily make thematic. This is at first striking because the sciences of language begin by excluding, according to Ricœur, expressivity, the saying of something about something, the reference and the manifesting functions of expressions. This exclusion is what he indicates by the "closed system of signs."

He enters this closed system of signs, to bring to light what the sciences of language presuppose. Changing the unity of language from the semiological to the semantic makes necessary a passage from structure to function. It also opens up two dimensions of the sign.

He reaches the heart of this consideration when he focuses on putting words together and selecting words. In order to put words together coherently, to select them from the whole system, a delimitation, a *dédoublement,* is necessary. This means that the problem of polysemy has a place even in the sciences of language. It also means that polysemy and symbolism belong to both the constitution and the function of every language. How does the word, put in relation to others, according to the science of language, derive its meaning? Surely, from its relation to other signs in the system with which it is connected. "So the possibility of symbolism is rooted in a function common to all words, in a universal function of language." (CI, 77-78) "When I speak, I realize only one part of the signifying potential; the remainder is obliterated by the total significance of the sentence which operates as the unity of speech." (CI, 72)

But this is only a partial answer, since it has not yet established the priority of semantics. It shows how symbolic function and polysemy are presupposed and belong to all language. It shows that it is the context, the sentence, which acts as the sifter of which meaning is meant. The further point Ricœur makes is that the meaning arrived at through or with this closed system of signs is not adequate. It does not do justice to the fullness of meaning. There is meaning still unaccounted for. It yields only an abstract language and an abstracted meaning. It yields the constitution of symbolics but not a semantics. Thus, there are two ways of giving an account of symbolism: by that which constitutes it, the elements, structures; and by that which it wants to say or to express.

This marks the break in the hierarchy of levels. The break is the different ways of considering the sign, the transition from semiology to semantics. The break is constituted by the closed system of signs of semiology. But the break is not an absolute as it might at first appear, for what Ricœur has done is to find semantics in semiology; and semiology in semantics – or, in other words, system and structure in speech, and meaning in structure. But to remain at the level of semiology and its meaning is unacceptable to Ricœur because he cannot accept the absoluteness of such a break. Therefore, the passage to the broader view of signs doing justice to the fuller meaning is necessary.

The same signs are seen from different levels. There are not two definitions of signs, but rather one expresses the relation to the sign in the system, and the other to its function in the sentence. (CI, 88) "To oppose the sign to sign, that is the semiological function; to represent the real by signs, that is the semantic function; and the first is subordinated to the second. The first is in view of the second, or if one wishes, it is in view of signifying or representative function that language is articulated." (CI, 248-249)

However, this so far has not settled the initial problem, the subordination of semiology and system to semantics and speech. The second part of the above quote has been well stated by Ricœur, but not yet established. How can that subordination be necessary? Can we just presume that the essence of language is to say something about something; that expressivity should not be left out of any consideration of language?

The clarification of this point demands a deepening in the view of polysemy. In approaching this question of polysemy as the "pivot of semantics" (CI, 91) from the side of synchrony, polysemy signifies in the system, and at a given moment a word has many meanings, which belong to the same state of the system. This view of polysemy misses the essential point, which is the process and history of usage. And that precisely is the crucial point.

Now this process of the transfer of meaning of metaphor presupposes new dimensions of meaning without loosing the old ones. It is this cumulative, metaphorical process which is projected over the surface of the system as polysemy. (CI, 93-94)

However, this expansion of sense, this history, is limited by the return to the system. "Words have more than one sense, but they do not have an infinite sense." (CI, 94) Thus, Ricœur has brought system into semantics, through this dialectic between expansion and limitation of meaning in system. But it brings out too the subordination of semiology to semantics, of synchrony to diachrony, at the semantic level. Both limitation and expansion are process, ". . . regulated polysemy is of the panchronic order, that is, both synchronic and diachronic to the degree that a history projects itself into states of systems, which henceforth are only instantaneous cross-sections in the process of sense, in the process of nomination." (CI, 94) Thus, the importance of the word as sign in the articulation of structure and of function is clear. However, it is the context which brings about the univocity or plurivocity of words in use or in discourse. The extent of the limitation of the semantic richness depends on the context. If the structure of a discourse allows several frames of reference, themes, topics, isotopies (CI, 94-95) then more than one interpretation of the multiple meanings is justified. But the crucial focal point is the word. Ricœur here brings tradition and history to the system, and system to process, to semantic flux. The priority of semantics over structure becomes clear, as well as the interrelation between them.

But this discussion is not yet adequate or complete. So far, Ricœur's attempt to bridge the gap between semiology and semantics and to subordinate semiology to semantics has been reflected on, but the two ways of taking the sign have not been seen in their polarity, except insofar as the *semiological perspective* is not sufficient by itself, and therefore cannot be considered the adequate and full treatment of sign or of language. "The semiological order does not constitute the total of language." (CI, 256) "Considered alone it is only the condition of articulation." (CI, 250)

Word

This calls for further reflection on the word as the point of articulation of the various levels of language. The articulation calls for a distinction of the sign in semiology or syntax, and the sign in semantics. On the one hand, the sign is "meaningless" in semiology, and on the other hand, it is word in semantics, "and words are the point of articulation of the semiological and the semantic in each event of speech." (CI, 93) We have already seen how Ricœur puts semantics into semiology, and at what price, i.e., the closure of the sign system; and we have seen how he puts semiology or system into semantics. We have also seen that semantics or (Ricœur's) phenomenology of language cannot accept the closure of the sign system, which is the overextension of a method and theory. Semiology can be considered to root the symbolic function and polysemy. This insight demands an adjustment in interpreting the relation between diachrony and synchrony, because of what Ricœur calls the surcharge of sense and the semantic regulation of the context. Further reflection on the closure of the sign system sees how the meaningful use of signs as words does not allow for a closed system, but rather demands an openness.

In attempting to evaluate the strength of the argument favoring the opening of the universe of signs, the distinction within the sign given above must be recalled. We saw that sign can be regarded from the point of view of its constitution, and the point of view of what it says, so that there are not two definitions. All Ricœur has said, then, is simply – yes – a sign is in a system. But that is not all it is. That does not do justice to or exhaust the full consideration of sign. We have already seen the subordination of semiology or system to function and to semantics. This allows for the opening of the sign system at a different but more essential level. At this higher level, signs have a reference function and a manifesting function. They point to and stand for things. They are expressions. As such they express, i.e., they show or reveal the world, and they manifest or posit the subject. The semiological sign system is a lower level which cannot do adequate justice to this aspect of sign. On this level, there is no saying of something, nor a positing of the I who appropriates language in speaking; the uniqueness of the I and the situation or occasion of the speaker and the speaking (e.g., tense, demonstratives) go beyond the limits of this level. Thus the closure of the sign system is not tenable on this level. And it is the more fundamental level, once the new unity of language in the sentence is accepted. Thus semantics gives the unity not only to the sentence, but to the sign. The dual nature of signs of the semiologist is superseded on this higher level by accepting the reference, that to which the sign points, as giving it unity.

Reduction, Signification, Subject

We must now return to a point made at the beginning of this chapter. We must attempt to consider this interarticulation and these views of sign from the point of view of the elements Ricœur considers central to any phenomenology: reduction, signification, and subject.

Semiology is a science of signs in system, indicating an essential aspect of sign and of language: i.e., that there is a difference, a distance constitutive of signs. This then is the transcendental of language, the condition of possibility of language. The separation, distance, difference, is the origin and commencement of a language. (CI, 253) It is the reduction!

But insofar as semiology deals with a closed system of language, it retains only one aspect, a first aspect of the reduction. By cutting off signification and the subject, it retains only the negative aspect of reduction. This reflects Ricœur's conviction that semiology does not constitute the total of language. (CI, 256) Nevertheless, insofar as it adheres to or guards this distance or separation, semiology can be considered "as the condition of possibility of the sign as such," giving rise to the transcendental character of the symbolic function.[6]

The other two aspects of reduction are the positive and the subjective. The positive aspect is the other side of the negative. It is the condition of the possibility of the reference. Thus, the reduction, considered in this second aspect, gives rise to signification, to the referring function of Husserl, to the saying of something about something. It, consequently, gives

[6] Paul Ricœur, "Philosophy of Language," pp. 28-29.

rise to the possibility of a poetics and an ontological language and to the bond with the world. But it is necessary to speak of a third aspect, the subjective aspect, as "the possibility of an ego to designate itself in the instance of discourse. Positivity and subjectivity go together, in the measure that the reference to the world and the reference to self, or as we say it above, the showing of a world and the positing of an ego, are symmetrical and reciprocal. (CI, 256) This is another aspect of language as expressive and is simply the manifesting function of an expression, which is the positing of an ego, "the subject installed by the reduction is nothing other than the beginning of a signifying life, the simultaneous birth of the spoken-being of the world and the speaking-being of man." (CI, 257) Thus the reduction, in its fuller sense, is this return to the self departing from its other which makes the transcendental not only of the sign, but of signification.

This makes clear how the symbolic function is transcendental. The negative aspect of reduction, the separation, is required in order to aim at what is separated. The separation gives rise to the other aspect, the referring. And since all language has the symbolic function as its root, as has been made clear, the signification given rise to by the reduction is fundamentally the symbolic function.

CONCLUSION

It has become clear what Ricœur meant by saying that if phenomenology is to survive it must come to grips with semiology. If it is to survive, phenomenology must somehow be able to put system in speech, and at the same time semantics in semiology. A theory of sign must be adequate to both aspects of signs: the constitutive and the functioning aspects.

Ricœur finds that (1) semiology has to be subordinated to semantics, but he must admit system into speech, and (2) symbolic function belongs to all language as the condition of possibility, presupposing reduction or separation; and it belongs to the constitution as well as the function of signification.

Thus, both phenomenology and semiology have had to make adjustments. Ricœur has tried to find the point of conversion of system and event, of structure and function. He has articulated these on the word as sign.

He thinks that this detour into the science of language has yielded a more precise notion of the symbolic function. (CI, 73) "The semantic basis thus mediated by the structural forms will become accessible to a more indirect comprehension but a more sure one."

That is why he speaks of beginning with science of language to arrive at a phenomenology of language. And the condition placed on the phenomenology of language must be constantly adhered to. Nevertheless, phenomenology, in its confrontation with semiology, must respond with a yes and a no. It accepts the condition of semiology; it even accepts semiology as its base, its foundation, giving its condition of possibility. But it cannot accept the absolutization of semiology; nor the closed system which springs from that absolutization; nor the limitation of language to a discrete object separate from speech. However, because he works through semiology and sees its limitations, does not mean Ricœur dismisses it. He does take it seriously and accepts the condition placed on phenomenology if it is to survive. But he thinks he has included that condition in his articulation of the different levels of language in his hierarchy of levels.

CHAPTER VIII

CONCLUSIONS

INTRODUCTION

Although various directions in Ricœur's development have been confronted and exposed, they have not been put up against the more general questions of his constancy and continuity, of the possibility and the nature of the pure reflection and eidetics of the will in general after its confrontation with Nabert, Freud, and semiology. From the beginning of this treatment the underlying intimation has been in favor of a certain fundamental continuity in the development of his philosophy of the will, not only in spite of his changes or deepening, but to some extent precisely because of his constant deepenings. Thus the explicit project of this concluding chapter becomes clear. This chapter therefore shall return to and recapture the development of this treatment to focus on the changes it captures. The return shall be more a synthesis than a summary.

EXTENSIONS OF LANGUAGE AND INTERPRETATION

Extensions and the philosophy of the will

Ricœur recently refers to his "dissatisfaction" [1] with the type of analysis of his *Le volontaire et l'involontaire*. In this return to his initial project, he indicates in general terms how he would now do this first stage. Several points should be explicated about this return, especially in relation to his more recent extensions.

First, he still refers to the first stage of the philosophy of the will as phenomenology. Thus it is clear that he is still in accord with the article "Phenomenology of Will and Action," in that a phenomenology of the

---

[1] Paul Ricœur, "The Problem of the Will and Philosophical Discourse," in *Patterns of the Life-World,* ed. by J. Edie, F. Parker, and C. Schrag, p. 273.

will is presupposed by psychoanalysis. He still wants to put that first in an overall philosophy of the will.

However, he explicitly mentions an extension. He refers to three types of discourse on the will, with the first as a phenomenological discourse. The extension he refers to is the extension from a phenomenology of the will to a phenomenological *discourse* on the will. What we notice is that all three types of treatment are discourses, even the phenomenological and first consideration. This means that all the types are on the level of language, and will therefore require some sort of interpretation of language, and presuppose a philosophy of language which allows for such an all-pervasive extension of language and language analysis. Before further treating language, several points about the first level should be further considered.

Phenomenological discourse on the will

These several points are: 1. that even this phenomenological level is already interpretation; 2. that this first level is not limited merely to the explicit phenomenology of Husserl or to phenomenologies of the will of the post-Husserlian phenomenologists, but is now open to Aristotle and the tradition which speaks and writes about the will; 3. that the dialectic of the *Le volontaire et l'involontaire* is also reorientated so that it is also aligned with language analysis.

That this first type of discourse on the will is interpretation, although not explicitly mentioned in this article as such, follows from the last few chapters of our study. It is also clear from other recent works of Ricœur.[2] We have already considered at great length the nature of reflective philosophy for interpretation. All reflection is interpretation. We have only indirect access to the meaning of our acts and to the meaning of ourselves. Reflection is an appropriation process. Reflective interpretation is also the appropriation of the depth meaning of texts of written discourse. This brings us to a further point.

Ricœur has now come to admit that even the great philosophers such as Aristotle, "have said something significant about the will." [3] And even

---

[2] Paul Ricœur, "Religion, Atheism, and Faith," in the *Religious Significance of Atheism*; "The Critique of Subjectivity and Cogito in the Philosophy of Heidegger," in *Heidegger and the Quest for Truth*, ed. by M. Frings; "What is a Text? Explanation and Interpretation," article at the end of *Mythic-Symbolic Language and Philosophical Anthropology*, by David M. Rasmussen. The first two of these appear in French translation in CI. These are not the only recent articles or lectures which bear this point out.

[3] Paul Ricœur, "Will and Philosophical Discourse," p. 273.

this phenomenological type of discourse extends back in history that far, although it has no phenomenological justification nor does it have a unity. The point is that he sees or interprets the texts of some great philosophers in such a way as to bring to light certain phenomenological aspects of the voluntary and the involuntary.

He still must, in the first context of phenomenological discourse, make room for Freud and his influence, which is one manifestation of the limits of a phenomenological discourse on will. This point will be further borne out in this chapter.

Still within this first type of discourse, Ricœur admits becoming more "attentive to the contribution of ordinary language analysis. . . ." [4] Such a confrontation between conceptual analysis and phenomenology reveals certain mutual overlaps and contributions of one to the other.

Saying and doing: a "new equilibrium"

Certain extensions relevant to language and the philosophy of the will have not yet been sufficiently explicated in terms of Ricœur's recent extensions, and in this context, as basic to these extensions. Ricœur in recent writings and lectures has referred to "A new equilibrium between saying and doing." [5] Not only must we understand that all reflection is interpretation, but from his lengthy study of semiology and theories of language analysis, we must also comprehend the new equilibrium in order to grasp the centrality of discourse. The new equilibrium is what makes all levels of a philosophy of the will to be types of discourse.

The "new equilibrium" is really an extension of saying (writing) so that it is fundamental instead of subordinate to action. This shows why and how all philosophy of will is discourse: because of what he refers to as the "connection" between desire to be and the power of the word.[6]

When we speak of the word as a living and effective word, we evoke a connection between the word and the active core of our existence. We imply that the word has the power to change the understanding we have of ourselves. Its power is not primarily imperative in nature, however. Before the word addresses itself to our will as an order and elicits obedience, it addresses itself to what I called our existence, and elicits effort and desire; it changes us, not because a will is imposed on our will but because of the effort made by "the hearing which understands." The word reaches us at the level of the symbolic structures of our existence, the dynamic schemes which express our way of understanding

---

[4] Paul Ricœur, in a preface to Don Ihde, *Hermeneutical Phenomenology*, p. XI.
[5] *Ibid.*
[6] Paul Ricœur, "Religion, Atheism and Faith," pp. 78-79.

our situation and of projecting our power in that situation. Our existence as
capable of being modified by the word is prior to the will, therefore, and even
prior to the principle of obligation, which according to Kant is the a priori
principle of the will. The inner connection between our desire to be and the
power of the word is a consequence of the act of listening, of hearkening, which
I discussed earlier. This connection in its turn makes possible will, evaluation,
decision, choice. These phenomena are only the surface projections of the
underlying relationship between our sense of situation, our understanding, and
our discourse, to refer again to the main notions in Heidegger's analysis of
Dasein.[7]

Note the power of the word. The word has a "mysterious" *power* over
us. It can change us because of our effort to hear which comprehends.
"The word reaches us at the level of the symbolic *structure* of our existence, the *dynamic schemes* which express our way of understanding our
situation and of projecting our powers in that situation." [8] The word
touches us at the core of our separation from our surroundings, but also
at the point at which we can relate in meaningful references to the world,
and thus express ourselves. This is at the heart of man. Hearing the word
from silent dwelling allows the "dynamic schemes" to remain dynamic
and alive instead of sterile and sedimented. Thus the word reaches the
dynamic core of existence and is able to change us. "Our existence as
capable of being modified by the word is prior to the will, therefore, and
even prior to the principle of obligation, which, according to Kant, is the
a priori principle of the will." [9]

Notice the priority of the word to the will and to formalistic ethics. It
is the inner connection between the power of the word and the desire to
be which makes will possible. And the most fundamental aspect of this
connection is its rootedness in hearing. Thus hearing the word becomes
crucial as a deepening of the receptivity which Ricœur has come to consider more and more an aspect of the openness of our existence. Our existence as effort to exist and desire to be is at its depth most fundamentally
related to a hearing of the word and a silence which changes us by allowing
us to comprehend ourselves in this process of coming to comprehend from
hearing.

In other recent writings,[10] Ricœur has expressed the power of the word,
its relation to being, and its openness in terms taken from Heidegger.[11]

---

[7] Paul Ricœur, "Religion, Atheism and Faith," pp. 78-79.
[8] *Ibid.*
[9] *Ibid.*, p. 79.
[10] CI, *passim,* especially in the articles collected in Part V, "Religion et Foi." Also
in "The Critique of Subjectivity and Cogito in the Philosophy of Heidegger," in
Heidegger and the Quest for Truth.
[11] Martin Heidegger, *Being And Time,* pp. 206-209.

Listening, hearing, and silence are existential possibilities which are thus a mode of being other than that of the ready-to-hand and is more fundamental than doing: "Listening ... is a mode of being which is not yet a mode of doing, and for this reason it escapes the alternatives of submission and revolt." [12] Listening, hearing, and reflective interpretation of a text are modes of being:

When a word says something, when it discloses not only something of beings but of Being – as in the case with the word of the poet or the thinker – we are confronted with what could be called a "word-event," a word process. Something is said of which I am not the origin, nor the owner. The word – unlike the tools of work and production, or goods to be consumed – is not at my disposal. In a word-event, I dispose of nothing, I do not impose myself. I am no longer the master. I am led beyond care and concern. In this situation of nonmastery lies the origin of both obedience and freedom.[13]

Ricœur goes on to follow Heidegger in rooting the comprehending hearing in silence. "Silence opens a space for hearing." This keeping silent for comprehending-hearing is not a dumb silence or a lack. Rather, it is because of a disclosedness of Being that there is silence. Silence is thus a "mode of discourse," [14] and as such, "it gives rise to a potentiality-for hearing which is genuine, and to a Being-with-one-another which is transparent.[15] Thus Ricœur, interpreting Heidegger, considers silence to be more fundamental than hearing and listening and to be their origin.

Thus we can obtain a subtle glimpse of the critique of subjectivity which is parallel to the challenge of subjectivity from semiology. The other side of the overthrowing of subjectivity as a mode of being belonging to a certain metaphysical age in which substance and subject come together is an hermeneutic of the "I am." [16] But the full elaboration of this interpretation and the full clarification of the power of the word which we do not master even as poets and thinkers, to which we as poets and thinkers are bound, requires a fuller illumination of the extensions of interpretation and the all pervasiveness of discourse which is fixed in writing. These clarifications are what we must turn to in order to comprehend Ricœur's recent shifts and reorientations. These extensions spring from the "new equilibrium" we have been reflecting on between saying and doing, as should be clear.

[12] Paul Ricœur, "Religion, Atheism and Faith," p. 71.
[13] *Ibid.*, p. 71-72.
[14] *Ibid.*, p. 74; a quote from Heidegger's *Being and Time*, p. 208.
[15] *Ibid.*
[16] Paul Ricœur, "Will and Philosophical Discourse," p. 288.

Interpretation and discourse

Again we come back to Ricœur's recent references to his extended views. Two such references are particularly relevant to introduce the context of his extensions of interpretation and discourse: "I call the first type phenomenological discourse (this already implies an extension of what I have previously called phenomenology)." [17] As we mentioned above, the importance of listening to the text of other philosophers who have interpreted and expressed the will is an extension. Ricœur wants to go back to the depth history by way of these texts; and let the texts speak and to appropriate the depth meaning of these texts; and he has included even in the first level or type of discourse as a phenomenology of the will the going back to the text. Thus, although in this article he does not explicitly say so, we have seen that even the phenomenology of the will is already interpretation, not only as phenomenology, but also as hermeneutic of a text. We will see the implicit hermeneutics of the phenomenology of the will of *Le volontaire et l'involontaire*. We must clarify what these types of discourse involve as discourses fixed in texts and necessitating a return to the texts of the great philosophers in the past. But before attempting such a clarification, we must focus briefly on another reference from Ricœur:

> I would even permit myself to note, in this context, that the hermeneutics which is anticipated is latently broader than that which is actually expressed in the *Symbolism of Evil and Freud and Philosophy*, where the idea of interpretation is still posed in a limited sense – too limited, I would say today – insofar as it is bound to the notion of symbol, of double meaning. If one takes the widest notion of a text as a guide on the hermeneutic level, instead of simply the notion of the signification of a double meaning, then one can say that the "dialectic of the diagnostic" directly anticipates this hermeneutics of a text – which is to say hermeneutics in the broad sense.[18]

We have already seen in the last chapter the need for these extensions in relation to the challenge of structuralism. Instead of defining hermeneutics or interpretation in relation to signification with a double meaning, he does so now with relation to the whole of language and in relation to a text. Thus the symbolic function and interpretation must be re-interpreted in this more fixed context of the text. From this recent deepening of insight, it is more clear how the whole project of the philosophy of the will is one type or level of interpretation, and to some extent, the various ways that this first level of discourse as phenomenology are already her-

---

[17] Paul Ricœur, "Will and Philosophical Discourse," p. 273.
[18] Paul Ricœur, Preface to Ihde, p. XVI.

meneutical. However, one further remark in relation to this broader view
of interpretation is in order before turning to the relation of the text to
interpretation.

Although Ricœur admits explicitly an extension and broadening view of
hermeneutics, and corrects the view of hermeneutics as limited to symbols,
he

> continues to hold that it is the condensation point and ... the place of greatest
> density, because it is in the symbol that language is revealed in its strongest force
> and with its greatest fullness. It says something independently of me, and it
> says more than I can understand. The symbol is surely the privileged place of
> the experience of the surplus of meaning.[19]

Ricœur refers to the dispossession of immediacy, which we have the-
matically considered above in the past few chapters [20] (*passim*), as having
its extreme form in the reading of a text and understanding the signs inscribed there.[21] However, we must explicate a point relevant to our treatment. This is the extreme form of dispossession and not the only form.
This insight allows us to grant that there are various interrelated modes of
interpreting signs inscribed in different and various forms of text. Comprehending this allows not only for the various modes of interpretation of
the first level of philosophy of the will, but also allows us to clarify certain
implicit directions of his initial treatment in *Le volontaire et l'involontaire*.
If we allow for a Ricœurian approach, we might speak of the polysemy of
text and see the unity of the different modes of interpreting, as well as the
diversity in the various uses, meanings and levels of meaning of the word
"text."

Discourse and text

We turn now to the fixing of discourse in writing. The written text gives
rise to explanation as a first mode of reading the text and to interpretation
as another mode of reading it. This whole analysis is similar to the interarticulation of a phenomenology of speech and structuralism although the
context is extended. Ricœur wants to interarticulate the semiological and
the hermeneutical approaches to a text; and both these approaches have
elements which we must employ if we are to listen and hear the text speak
in the various types of discourse on the will. This bringing together of two
modes of reading the text reveals a depth semantics not obvious without to
some extent a structural explanation of the text; the interpretative reading

---

[19] Paul Ricœur, Preface to Ihde, pp. XVI-XVII.
[20] *Passim*.
[21] Paul Ricœur, Preface to Ihde, p. XV.

of the text is able to appropriate the depth semantics. In order to clarify this complementarity of structural explanation and interpretation on the level of a text we shall follow briefly some of the points of Ricœur's own exposition: 1. first dealing with some aspects of the text; 2. then with the structural approach; 3. and with interpretation; 4. then, an inter-articulation; 5. and finally, apply this "new" definition of interpretation to the extensions of his project of a philosophy of the will.

It is necessary for us to comprehend with Ricœur some aspects of a text in order to interrelate the different modes of reading the text. One of the aspects he heavily emphasizes is that a text fixes discourse by writing. There are two important points here: the fixation and the writing. What is fixed by the writing is a discourse. And it is written precisely as not spoken, i.e., the written text is not merely another mode of speaking. Yet the writing is a parallel to the speaking. Thus, as speaking is related to listening, so writing is related to reading. "For the time being, let us say that the reader takes the place of the listener, just as writing takes the place of speaking." [22] However, the writing-reading relation is not a dialogue, or particularization of speaking-listening. This is because of the fixation of discourse in the text. Because discourse becomes fixed in the writing it is liberated from speech. "This liberation of writing whereby it gets substituted for speech is the birth of a text." [23] But, as we shall see later, this moment of the birth of the text as liberation and substitution is also the moment of cutting off the discourse which becomes fixed by writing from the reference which makes discourse meaningful as saying something about something to someone, in which I express myself in expressing these references. This intrinsically relates to what we have dealt with in the last chapter as reduction in relation to language, with its negative, positive, and subjective aspects. Ricœur here will similarly inter-articulate structural explanation and interpretation as two modes of reading by implicitly relating to these levels of reduction. The difference between discourse as speech and discourse fixed in a text is that the fixation by writing, the liberation of substitution, allows for the separation and the distance or difference of the negative moment of reduction in a more explicit manner than was considered as belonging to all language in the last chapter. In speech these references are more readily seen to be open and not cut off, since language is open and not a closed system of signs. But what happens when the text substitutes for speech is that these references are suspended or cut off. But . . . "a text, we shall see, is not without

22 Paul Ricœur, "What is a Text?", p. 136.
23 *Ibid.*, p. 137.

references; it will be precisely the task of reading, as interpretation, to actualize the references. At least, in this suspension wherein reference is deferred, in the sense that it is postponed, a text is somehow "in the air," outside of the world or without a world; by means of this obliteration of all relation to the world, every text is free to enter into relation with all other texts which come to take the place of the circumstantial reality shown by living speech." [24]

There are three moments to be considered, then, before returning to our initial project of relating this reading to the three types of discourse of a philosophy of the will: 1. the explanation of a text by structuralism; 2. the interpretive reading of the text; 3. and the reconciliation of these two in relation to a *depth semantics* which can be appropriated and reactivated or re-enacted.

The first type of reading of a text is its explanation "by means of its internal relation, its structure." [25] This is the suspension, the abstraction from reference to turn within the text without an external. The reference to the world and to subjectivities or intersubjectivity is cut off or bracketed. What is focused on in this structural analysis is the internal relations or "an interplay of relations." [26]

Similarly, a mytheme is not one of the sentences of a myth but an oppositive value attached to several individual sentences forming, in the terminology of Levi-Strauss, a "bundle of relations": "It is only in the form of a combination of such bundles that the constitutive unities acquire a meaning-function. What is here called meaning-function is not all what the myth means, its philosophical or existential content or intention, but the arrangement, the disposition of mythemes, in short, the structure of the myth.

Ricœur admits that this type of analysis explains the text but does not interpret it. What he means is that there is a suspension of meaning, a bracketing or closure to the positive aspect of reduction as reference within language, and here, within the text. This would be actualized in a recitation of the myth (Oedipus, in this treatment). This suspension allows for the taking of the text in isolation from any situation of discourse, and for a "postponement of all actualization by present speech." [27]

A new concept of interpretation

Before turning to reconcile interpretative reading of a text with the above

---

[24] Paul Ricœur, "What is a Text?", p. 137.
[25] *Ibid.*, p. 138.
[26] *Ibid.*, p. 141.
[27] *Ibid.*, p. 142.

structural explanatory reading of a text, Ricœur considers a "new" concept of interpretation, which highlights his full extension of this concept from his former or narrow view limiting interpretation to double meanings, or moving from one level of meaning to another, and only in relation to symbols. He briefly highlights the two different modes of reading thus: [28]

Two ways of reading, we have said, are offered to us. By reading we can prolong and reinforce the suspension affecting the text's reference to the environment of a world and the audience of speaking subjects; this is the explanatory attitude. But we can also bring an end to this suspension and complete the text in actual discourse. It is this second attitude which is the genuine aim of reading. The other sort of reading would not even be possible if it were not first of all apparent that the text, as writing, waits and calls for a reading; if a reading is possible, it is indeed because the text is not closed in on itself but open out onto something else. By any supposition reading is a linking together of a new discourse to the discourse of the text. The linking reveals, in the very constitution of the text, an original capacity of being reenacted, which is its open character. Interpretation is the concrete result of this openness and of this linking together.

Thus, interpretation is considered to be an appropriation of the discourse of the text, as actualizing or reenacting it. This appropriation has three moments: a. Ricœur means by appropriation first that in such interpretation of the text there is also a self-interpretation. In this moment we see the reflective character of hermeneutics. "Hermeneutics and reflective philosophy are there correlative and reciprocal." [29] b. Appropriation also means the making proper or my own, which overcomes cultural distance of the foreign. It is no longer foreign, but now my own. c. Most important, this process of interpretation as appropriation is actualization or re-enactment. He compares reading to performing a musical score, in that in reading, we actualize "the semantic virtualities of the text." [30] Interpretation in this sense becomes like speech in that it achieves the writing: "the actualized text finds at last an environment and an audience, a world and intersubjective dimension." [31] Thus this type of reading "achieves the discourse of the text in a dimension similar to speech." [32] It to some extent reactivates what was fixed by the writing as a fixed discourse and releases it to the extent that it is appropriated as actualized.

[28] Paul Ricœur, "What is a Text?", p. 144.
[29] *Ibid.*, p. 145.
[30] *Ibid.*
[31] *Ibid.*, p. 146.
[32] *Ibid.*, p. 145.

Reconciliation of the opposition

Ricœur now proceeds, in a typical Ricœurian style, to attempt to reconcile these now obviously opposed modes of reading a text. We have already at least implicitly seen the direction of such a reconciliation. All that remains is to explicitate it briefly, before returning to our basic theme of this section.

Ricœur shows the failure of the first concept of both structuralism and interpretation, as the first step in bringing about a reconciliation in these two modes of reading a text. Structuralism as such has too formal or abstract a conception of sense (or meaning). "We tried to hold ourselves to a notion of sense (or meaning) which would be strictly reducible to the arrangement of the elements within the text. As a matter of fact no one remains with a conception as formal as this of the sense (or meaning) of a narrative or myth." [33] In fact, this type of formal approach presupposes this fuller sense or meaning. In attempting to overcome the contradiction, the myth expresses the contradiction in meaningful relationship. Ricœur holds that it is impossible to bracket or exclude the function of the myth "as a narrative of the origins." [34] Rather, structural analysis allows us to be withdrawn from a superficial reading of the text, brackets the superficial semantics, "that of the apparent narrative, so as to make manifest a *depth-semantics,* which is the latent narrative." Thus through structural analysis of the text we are brought from a naive or superficial interpretation of a text to a depth or critical interpretation. But what does this do to his initial concept of interpretation as appropriation?

What this actually does for interpretation as appropriation is to postpone such an appropriation to let the text speak, to allow the text and its language to interpret first. The concept of the first level of interpretation, then, is now an "objective interpretation" [35] which postpones the subjective or other end of the arch of hermeneutics. The reader must let the interpreting text have its say before too quickly appropriating it and reactualizing or enacting it. Thus structural analysis has extended the initial (subjective) concept of interpretation, to admit a separation or bracketing of the reference of the supposed intentions and references of the author, and allows the reader to focus on and hear what the text itself wants to say and let it orientate our thinking according to it and its direction. "The sense of the text is the direction which it opens up for our thought." Ricœur goes on to repeat this new definition of interpretation:

[33] Paul Ricœur, "What is a Text?", p. 146.
[34] *Ibid.,* p. 147.
[35] *Ibid.,* p. 149.

This concept of sense as direction for thought leads us to a new definition of interpretation which would be less a subjective operation than an objective process; less an act on the text, than an act *of* the text. This process of interpretation has something to do with the depth semantics of the text delivered by structural analysis; it is this depth semantics which is to understand in dynamic terms; whereas the structure constitutes the statics of the text, the depth semantics is itself a process of meaning; it requires a fresh interpretation because it is itself an interpretation, it is interpretation which I called the act of the text.[36]

This new understanding of interpretation does not eliminate the idea of it as appropriation, but only postpones it until the end of the process. "It is the other end of what we have called the hermeneutical arch: it is the last pillar of the bridge, the anchor of the arch in the soil of lived experience." [37] What the reader must do, then, is enter the process of the text, and let it first interpret and reveal the process of depth meaning, before appropriation by "re-saying" as "re-enacting." This latter is the level of hermeneutic at the end of the arch; as Ricœur calls it, "the anchor of the arch in the soil of lived experience." Thus the objective interpretation necessitates a postponement of the subjective interpretation.

This is precisely what Ricœur seems to wish to do now in the re-orientation of his project of a philosophy of the will. He wants to consider different types of discourse fixed in texts, go to those with an interpretative reading. This interpretative reading must be objective first, or a hearing of the word of the text, then, an appropriation of that word of the text. But he has called the first type of such discourse, as we have seen, a phenomenological discourse (of decision, preference, choice, etc.). How is this a phenomenological discourse? And what is the limit of such a type of discourse?

Ricœur now considers the whole level of phenomenology of the will to be discourse and therefore to require some level of interpretation. This meets the analysis and development of reflection of our last few chapters. There we found that all reflection is indirect and a reading of signs, and therefore is interpretation. And the most extensive signs are those expressed in language. However, in speaking of all levels of the philosophy of the will as discourse, we must not presume that all interpretation is of the same kind and on the same level. The ultimate will arise from his poetics of the will. But we should realize that the reading of the texts of the great philosophers, as we have seen, requires all that we have said about the reconciliation of explanation and interpretation in reading the

[36] Paul Ricœur, "What is a Text?", p. 148.
[37] *Ibid.,* p. 150.

text, which lets the text speak for itself before appropriating it into the soil of subjective lived experience. But the first and guiding type of discourse is discourse about the subjective will, the will experienced in decision, preference, choice, etc. This phenomenological discourse gives rise to interpretative reading which will meet Husserl and the post-Husserlian writers on the will, such as Ricœur himself, and let their texts speak for themselves, about subjective will. In drawing out the relation between the voluntary and involuntary, it again will be necessary to "read" Freud; and to incorporate a conceptual analysis, and all this on the level of phenomenological discourse on the will.

But in turning to the second type of discourse, that discourse on meaningful actions, Ricœur is indicating an attempt to read the texts of the objective will, thus showing a further extension of his philosophy of the will, as well as the limits of a phenomenology and eidetic approach. He is trying to appropriate the process of meaning of the expressed will. As Husserl was the chief representative of the phenomenological type of discourse, Hegel is the chief representative of this type.[38]

In the transition from phenomenological discourse to discourse about meaningful action, Ricœur points out that phenomenological discourse on the will is only an aspect of a broader type of discourse,[39] that discourse about meaningful action. This broader dimension is the objective will, what Hegel calls objective mind.[40]

These two types of discourse on the will point to a third type of discourse on the will which is a "discourse in the form of interpretation, which recognizes behind the changes happening in the two previous fields the depth history of the mode of being in which being itself is both concrete and disclosed." [41] These types of discourse thus recognize in human activity "the character of being as act," and is "an approach to the basis of being as creativity." [42]

Ricœur has only indicated in rough sketch in recent articles and lectures the contours of this type of discourse as interpretation and how it must deal with the problem of a broken discourse, of the many ways in which being manifests itself. However, these problems are not the immediate focus of our treatment and it is better to leave this profound level of consideration and return to our problematics.

We must at this point meet head-on another of our initial questions

[38] Paul Ricœur, "Will and Philosophical Discourse," p. 279.
[39] *Ibid.,* p. 277.
[40] *Ibid.,* p. 281.
[41] *Ibid.,* p. 289.
[42] *Ibid.,* p. 283.

about the first project of a phenomenology of the will; to what extent is it still viable, as an eidetics, and to what extent has Ricœur already been hermeneutical even in *Le volontaire et l'involontaire* and his earlier works on the will? We have already seen to what extent he wishes to extend interpretation, symbol, and to deepen and broaden his initial philosophy of the will. We have also seen the basic contours of a return to the initial project. But now, tersely put, we should fulfill this return by considering a last level; the question of what is already implicit in the first stage, and to what extent that first stage is still considered to be necessary.

EXTENSIONS AND EIDETICS

Necessity of an eidetics

In spite of those changed views of the nature of reflection, Ricœur still wants to consider the eidetic not only to be possible but to be necessary. This can be made clear from several considerations on the articles "Phenomenology of Will and Action" and "Will and Philosophical Discourse." First of all, the first of these articles is divided into three parts: the first part is a philosophical setting up of the question; the second is a phenomenology of the will, and the third is the psychopathology and its confrontation with phenomenology of the will, especially relating to the question of motivation. The point of importance for us here is that Ricœur not only has considered the phenomenology of the will first, but maintained that it must be first; and that the psychoanalysis must presuppose such a phenomenology.[43]

The very fact that Ricœur presents the phenomenology of the will in the position in which he does, and does so deliberately, and not simply arbitrarily, indicates that he still considers it a guideline and a prerequisite. He mentions several points concerning the nature of such an eidetic phenomenology of the will and what it owes to Husserl, stressing intentionality, description and imaginative variation. Then, in working out the intentional analysis and description of essential structures, beginning with the *noema* and then going to the description of the noetic or correlative acts, he insists on the intentionality or reference as well as the self-imputation of the subject. This is precisely the point he insists on in *Le volontaire et l'involontaire* (12) and works out throughout the whole book, in focusing on the relation of the voluntary and the involuntary. Thus it is clear that Ricœur definitely has in mind in this analysis an eidetic analysis of a similar

---

[43] Paul Ricœur, "Will and Philosophical Discourse," p. 275; also "Phenomenology of Will and Action," p. 118-119.

character as that of *Le volontaire et l'involontaire*. However, it must immediately be added that this is definitely a post-Freudian phenomenology of the will, as will become clear later. But in spite of all the changes and challenges he still returns to the same themes and in a similar fashion as in *Le volontaire et l'involontaire*.

Not only that, but, in spite of the changed view from the emphasis of *Le volontaire et l'involontaire* concerning the voluntary as the total source of the meaning of willing, and as giving the meaning to the involuntary, which then becomes human from the voluntary's taking it up, Ricœur still considers the need to study or focus *first* on the voluntary and intentionality. This becomes clear from a text from this article: [44]

In determining something, I determine myself. Thus I myself figure in the project as the one to whom the action can be imputed. It is perhaps at this point that the *privileged character of voluntary intention appears*. Indeed, it is in the voluntary intention that the relation between the self and its acts is revealed in all its plenitude. Every act, in the strong sense of the term, possesses at the same time an objective intending and a relation of "imputation" which appears clearly in a decision; in making up my mind, I impute to myself the action, that is, I place it in a relation to myself such that, from then on, this action represents me in the world;

The intentional analysis reveals the self-imputation, which is the point in which action, or more precisely, my motives, represent me in the world and are the signs of my deeds. "Thus I posit myself as the agent in the intending of the action to be done." [45] This self-imputation is a pre-reflective imputation. This is a practical affirmation of such a character that it is in my deeds that I affirm myself. This, as we shall see, is the point of junction between phenomenology and psychoanalysis. And this also reveals the implicit hermeneutics of *Le volontaire et l'involontaire,* for, as Ricœur says here, in a way he could not have said it before his detour into Freud, "It is even (and only) on the basis of this pre-reflective affirmation of myself in my projects that all my judgements of reflection can be understood." [46] The above passage therefore reveals at the same time the intention of Ricœur to remain constant to the privileged character of voluntary intention, and therefore of intentional analysis, and also his change from the writing of *Le volontaire et l'involontaire,* so that now he sees the self-imputation in a slightly different light. Now it reveals the self-imputation as bringing to light the positing of my self, of a power-to-be. Thus

[44] Paul Ricœur, "Phenomenology of Will and Action," pp. 18-19.
[45] *Ibid.*, p. 19.
[46] *Ibid.*

the positing of the to be of myself is not limited to the voluntary, to effort, but is already in what is received.

The necessity of the phenomenology of the will becomes clear in yet another section of this short article. Again, for emphasis, it is necessary to quote Ricœur: "On the one hand psychoanalysis cannot exclude the phenomenology of volition, for it presupposes it at every turn." [47] This is more or less the same thing he says in *De l'interprétation*. All the terms and concepts of psychoanalysis, especially those which are negative, presuppose the terms revealed by a phenomenology. Every not-willing, not being free, presupposes the willing, the whole field of volition. Ricœur sees psychoanalysis referring to phenomenology both as therapy and as theory. As we pointed out in our chapter four, Freud's analysis presupposes or is implicitly aiming at a cure or a healing and therefore allows for the synthesis or for some teleology. There is the task of becoming conscious. "In this sense the analytic experience finds its finality in an implied phenomenology of volition." [48] And if this is the case on the therapeutic level, it has to be so at least implicitly on the level of theory. Thus it is clear that Ricœur considers a phenomenology of the will both possible and necessary, and presupposed for and by psychoanalysis.

Deepening of eidetics

In considering the limits of the eidetic method in chapter two, it has been explicitly pointed out that after the first chapter of each of the three parts of *Le volontaire et l'involontaire* the brackets had to be lifted since otherwise it would be impossible to approach the involuntary. After the eidetic descriptions the structures of the involuntary which were necessary to the voluntary from the eidetic description must be further clarified. In dealing with that level, and in order to have further access to it, Ricœur engaged in a *diagnostic* relation with the objective sciences. This use of the sciences as an aid in coming to a clearer understanding of the structures of the involuntary allowed Ricœur then to move from the objective grasp of these structures to the grasp of these structures in the lived body and the subjective involuntary.

But now, "an hermeneutical method, coupled with reflection," (DI, 443) can go a lot further than such an eidetic method. After learning from Nabert that all reflection is interpretation, and after turning to Freud, Ricœur has seen to what extent the *Cogito* is rooted in the desire. The un-

[47] Paul Ricœur, "Phenomenology of Will and Action," p. 30.
[48] *Ibid.,* p. 30.

conscious also is the source of meaning, and the *Cogito* is posited even before consciousness. This deepening is not all accessible to direct reflection, but only to a mediated reflection, an interpretation of signs and symbols. Whereas phenomenology can bring us to the original ground, a hermeneutic is necessary to reveal the full depths of this ground, the meaning of motives and of the subject which is not accessible to direct reflection. Thus the full meaning of our acts, of deeds, of effort, of desire, comes to light only with this coupling of reflection with hermeneutic. This precisely is the decentering which has been called for in order to reach the real meaning of consciousness.

The difference between the later view of motive and that of the earlier comes to light in its relation to choice as support. Ricœur now sees that the meaning of motives is rooted in desire. This insight into desire as positing is not accessible to immediate consciousness. The passivity or the receptivity which Ricœur indicated in each of the phases of the voluntary in *Le volontaire et l'involontaire* is considered as a receptivity of motives for choice, but now he clearly sees that it is the receptivity of motives as the reason for and inclination of the voluntary. It is clear then, that . . . "there is a point of passivity or of receptivity in the heart of volition by which will renders itself sensitive to anything which can incline it without necessitating it, which can provide it with an impulsion and a legitimization." [49]

It becomes more and more clear what Ricœur has in mind when he says that consciousness must lose itself in order to find itself, and that consciousness is a task. The effect on phenomenology of this insight is that phenomenology must be extended to a new field, or even cease to be phenomenology to come to the real and deeper meaning of consciousness. This is the only way of arriving at the deeper intelligibility, that of the unconscious, to arrive at the sense and its founding force which come to the representation and thus reach expression.

Thus the phenomenology of motivation is merely the "historical transposition of the system of instinctual vicissitudes; in particular, conscious motivation . . . is merely a secondary elaboration, a rationalization." [50] It is precisely this extension of motivation which required the extension beyond phenomenology. And the link between phenomenology and psychoanalysis making this extension from phenomenology possible is hermeneutics.[51] This interpretation is the means of making the necessary transition to the hidden meaning from the unconscious and inaccessible to immediate

---

[49] Paul Ricœur, "Philosophy of Will and Action," p. 24.
[50] *Ibid.*, p. 29.
[51] *Ibid.*, p. 31.

consciousness. When phenomenology opened the way to this area of motive and all that the volition is receptive to, it also opened the door to the extension of motivation, and to hermeneutics as access to this deeper meaning and intention not linked to consciousness.

Is it possible to say that Ricœur in *Le volontaire et l'involontaire* did not reach this level in his considerations on motivation and desire? The question rephrased is, to what extent and how did he (implicitly?) make this deepening in the first presentation of the phenomenology of the will?

Implicit hermeneutics of eidetics

If Ricœur did in the first treatment of the eidetic level reach the extended realm of motivation, then his phenomenology at that level can be said to have been implicitly hermeneutical. However, the question can be extended and then applied to the eidetic level. In considering the possibility of an implicit hermeneutics the above is not the only direction to be taken, but several others lie open and must be rendered explicit. Keeping in mind that Freud's is not the first influence, but Nabert's, it is possible to alter the context.

If we approach Ricœur's eidetic stage not only from the Freudian influence, can we not gain some insight into another possibility of an implicit hermeneutics? Chapter six has already brought this out to some extent, and also has explicitly worked out some of the hermeneutics on that level regarding the role of motivation in interpreting the meaning of acts. Is this not also a possible direction to take in working out the question of an implicit interpretation even in the treatment of *Le volontaire et l'involontaire*? Ricœur himself seems to allow for this interpretation of his earlier works. He does this when he says that all understanding of structures is already interpretation, and insists on the necessity of an interpretation between structural and hermeneutical understanding, one as presupposing the other. (CI, 64) Also, does not this structural understanding presuppose the hermeneutical understanding as an event?

Thus we have open to us two avenues of approach to the question of the implicit hermeneutics of the eidetic level. And it is not a question of taking one or the other, but both must be considered. First, the more general question of understanding as reflection according to Nabert's influence on Ricœur, would show that any understanding of deeds or events or acts is already interpretation or presupposes an hermeneutics. Second, the Freudian approach as it has influenced Ricœur would show that even in the first eidetics Ricœur has already implicitly dealt with the hidden meaning of acts, the hidden motives and the rooting and positing of the subject in desire.

Hermeneutics of hidden meaning

However, when we approach the question of the hidden motives, it is necessary to admit that Ricœur did not grasp this aspect of motives of Freud at the time of *Le volontaire et l'involontaire*. Therefore, this role of hermeneutics is the legacy of Freud and the result of his intense study of Freud. But in his whole approach to the involuntary he at least left this avenue open. For his diagnostic approach to the involuntary is not too far removed from the hermeneutics which he considers today as a necessary intermediary between eidetics or phenomenology of willing, and psychoanalysis. This therefore is a new dimension of hermeneutics which goes beyond what he has learned from Nabert. It is not sufficient to say that all understanding is hermeneutics of signs, because these signs are first deceptive, illusory. To be disillusioned it is necessary to pass through the hermeneutics of the deeper meaning of motives as signs of acts and deeds and reach toward the hermeneutics of the I am. But as he says in *De l'interprétation* (509), the illusion of Freud, Marx and Nietzsche are only secondary. Kant came closer to the fundamental illusion. It is necessary not to objectify the fundamental *arche* and *telos* in order to avoid making idols of them. And the hermeneutics of suspicion are needed to prevent this.

... the movement by which man empties himself in transcendence is second in relation to the movement by which he masters the Totally-Other to objectify it and dispose of it; for it is to master it that he projects himself there, in order to fill the emptiness of his ignorance. (DI, 509)

Ricœur's main concern in the *Le volontaire et l'involontaire* was to open the way to considering the realm of motives in phenomenology, i.e., as from the subjective point of view, as from the lived or owned body. In this endeavor, he opened the door for his later considerations, even though he did not see the depth that his later works would go after his study of Nabert and Freud. In fact, his treatment of Freud in *Le volontaire et l'involontaire,* which he has radically changed, reflects much of the influence of freudians and less of Freud himself. But once he attempts to articulate the phenomenological and the scientific readings of motives and the body, he lays the foundation for his own later work, which specifies this work and brings it to greater depth. But it would be an injustice to his later works to read too much of his later deepening in the early treatment of the eidetics of the will. Therefore it is necessary to admit that he did not see the full extent of the hidden aspect of motives; nor the rooting of motives in desire or life; nor the source of meaning from the involuntary; nor the central rule of silence as a mode of discourse; nor the full extent of his later critique of subjectivity.

CONCLUSION

It is clear enough at this point that some of the questions posed in chapter one cannot be answered by an unequivocal yes or no. Ricœur has definitely extended his views on some essential points. This was stated even in the first chapter. But as was also said there, such alterations in an author's development do not militate against the continuity and constancy in his development. And this constancy can be read in several ways. On the one hand, an attempt can be made to show the *constant elements* that have either remained the same throughout the development or have deepened by extention. On the other hand, the attempt can be made to see the later positions as already entailed in the first stages. This is what we have tried to do throughout this work. But we have also found that Ricœur has undergone some changes in central positions which cannot be considered merely as becoming explicit or as extensions. Throughout the unfolding of this work it has become clear to what extent Ricœur's philosophy even at the level of pure reflection is hermeneutical.

SELECTED BIBLIOGRAPHY

A. WORKS OF RICOEUR

"The Antinomy of Human Reality and the Problem of Philosophical Anthropology." *Readings in Existential Phenomenology*. Edited by Nathaniel Lawrence and Daniel O'Connor. New York: Prentice-Hall, 1967.

Le conflit des interprétations, Essais sur Herméneutique. Editions du Seuil, 1969.

"The Critique of Subjectivity and Cogito in the Philosophy of Heidegger." *Heidegger and the Quest for Truth*. Edited by Manfred S. Frings. Chicago: Quadrangle Books, 1968.

De l'interprétation: Essai sur Freud. Paris: Editions du Seuil, 1965.

"Existence et Herméneutique." *Interpretation der Welt, Festschrift für R. Guardini*. Edité par H. Kuhn, H. Kahlefeld et K. Forster. Wurzburg, 1965.

Fallible Man. Translated by Charles Kelbley. Chicago: Henry Regnery Company.

Freedom and Nature: The Voluntary and the Involuntary. Translated by Erazim Kohak. Evanston: Northwestern University Press, 1966.

"The Hermeneutics of Symbols and Philosophical Reflections." *International Philosophical Quarterly*, II (May, 1962), 191-218.

Histoire et Verité. Paris: Editions du Seuil, 1955.

History and Truth. Translated by Charles A. Kelbley. Evanston: Northwestern University Press, 1965.

Husserl: An Analysis of His Phenomenology. Translated by Edward G. Ballard and Lester E. Embree. Evanston: Northwestern University Press, 1967.

"Husserl and Wittgenstein." *Phenomenology and Existentialism*. Edited by Lee and Mandelbaum. Baltimore: Johns Hopkins University Press, 1967.

"Méthodes et tâches d'une phénoménologie de la volonté." *Problèmes actuels de la phénoménologie*. Edited by H. L. Van Breda. Paris: Desclée de Brouwer, 1952.

"New Developments in Phenomenology in France: The Phenomenology in France: The Phenomenology of Language." *Social Research*, XXXIV (1967), 1-30.

Philosophie de la volonté, Vol. I. *Le volontaire et l'involontaire*. Paris: Aubier, 1950.

Philosophie de la volonté, Vol. II. *Finitude et culpabilité,* Part I: *L'Homme faillible.* Paris: Aubier, 1960.

Philosophie de la volonté, Vol. II. *Finitude et culpabilité,* Part II: *La symbolique du mal.* Paris: Aubier, 1960.

"Philosophy of Will and Action." *Phenomenology of Will and Action.* Edited by Erwin W. Straus and Richard M. Griffith. Pittsburgh: Duquesne University Press, 1967.

Preface to *The Notion of the A Priori.* Mikel Dufrenne. Translated by Edward Casey. Evanston: Northwestern University Press, 1966.

Preface to *Hermeneutical Phenomenology.* Don Ihde. Evanston: Northwestern University Press, 1971.

"The Problem of the Will and Philosophical Discourse." *Patterns of the Life-World.* Edited by James M. Edie, Francis H. Parker and Calvin O. Schrag. Evanston: Northwestern University Press, 1970.

Quelques figures contemporaines. Appendice à *L'Histoire de la Philosophie Allemande,* par Emile Brehier. Edit. Vrin, 1955.

"Religion, Atheism, and Faith." *The Religious Significance of Atheism.* Alasdair Macintyre and Paul Ricœur. New York and London: Columbia University Press, 1969.

"Structure et Herméneutique." *Esprit* (November, 1963), 596-627.

"Structure-Word-Event." *Philosophy Today,* XII (Summer, 1968), 114-129.

"The Symbol . . . Food for Thought." *Philosophy Today,* IV (Fall, 1960), 196-207.

The Symbolism of Evil. Translated by Emerson Buchanan. New York: Harper & Row, 1967.

"The Unity of the Voluntary and the Involuntary as a Limiting Idea." *Readings in Existential Phenomenology.* Edited by Nathaniel Lawrence and Daniel O'Connor. New Jersey: Prentice-Hall, 1967.

"What is a Text? Explanation and Interpretation," an article at the end of *Mythic-Symbolic Language and Philosophical Anthropology,* David M. Rasmussen. The Hague: Martinus Nijhoff, 1971.

B. BIBLIOGRAPHIES

Vansina, Dirk F. "Bibliographie de Paul Ricœur (Jusqu'au juin 1962)." *Revue Philosophique de Louvain* (Août, 1962), 394-413.

"Bibliographie de Paul Ricœur (jusqu'à la fin de 1967)." *Revue Philosophique de Louvain.* (Février, 1968), 85-101.

C. OTHER WORKS

Bachelard, Suzanne. *A Study of Husserl's Formal and Transcendental Logic.* Evanston: Northwestern University Press, 1968.

Barret, William and Aiken, Henry, ed. *Philosophy in the Twentieth Century,* Vol. II. New York: Random House, 1962.

150   SELECTED BIBLIOGRAPHY

Barthel, Pierre. *Interprétation du Langage Mythique et Théologie Biblique.* Leiden: E. J. Brill, 1967.
Breton, Stanislas. "From Phenomenology to Ontology," *Philosophy Today,* Vol. IV (Winter, 1960), 227-37.
Cassirer, Ernst. *The Philosophy of Symbolic Forms.* Translated by Ralph Manheim. New Haven & London: Yale University Press, 1953.
Derrida, Jacques. *La voix et le phénomène: Introduction au problème du signe.* Paris: Presses Universitaires de France, 1967.
Doz, André. "L'Ontologie fondamentale et le problème de la culpabilité," *Revue de Métaphysique et de Morale.* LXI (1956), 661-95.
Dufrenne, Mikel. *Language & Philosophy.* Translated by Henry B. Veatch. Bloomington: Indiana University Press, 1963.
Farber, Marvin. *The Foundation of Phenomenology.* New York: Paine-Whitman Publishers, 1962.
Freud, Sigmund. *Moses and Monotheism.* Ed. by K. Jones. Vintage Books, Random House.
—. *The Standard Edition of the Complete Psychological Works of Sigmund Freud,* Translated by James Slachey. London: The Hargrath Press, 1966.
Hackett, Stuart C. "Philosophical Objectivity and Existential Involvement in the Methodology of Paul Ricœur." *International Philosophical Quarterly,* IX (1968), 11-39.
Hamburg, Carl. *Symbol and Reality.* Martinus Nijhoff: The Hague, 1956.
Harries, Karsten. "Heidegger and Hölderlin: The Limits of Language." *Personalist,* XLIV (1963), 5-23.
Hartman, Klaus. "Phenomenology, Ontology, and Metaphysics." *The Review of Metaphysics,* XXII (September, 1968), 85-112.
Heidegger, Martin. *Being and Time.* Translated by John Macquarrie & Edward Robinson. New York and Evanston: Harper & Row, 1962.
—. *Kant and the Problem of Metaphysics.* Translated by James S. Churchill. Bloomington: Indiana University Press, 1962.
—. *Sein und Zeit.* Max Niemeyer Verlag: Tübingen, 1963.
Husserl, Edmund. *Ideas.* Translated by W. R. Boyce Gibson. New York: Collier Books, 1962.
—. *Ideen zu einer reinen Phänomenologie und Phänomenologischen Philosophie.* Herausgegeben von Marly Biemel. Haag: Martinus Nijhoff, 1962.
—. *Idées directrices pour une phénoménologie pure.* Introduction, traduction et commentaire par Paul Ricœur. Paris: Gallimard, 1950.
—. *Logische Untersuchungen.* Max Niemeyer Verlag: Tübingen, 1968.
—. "Phenomenology." *Encyclopedia Britannica,* 14 ed., Vol. IV, 699-702.
—. *Recherches Logiques.* Tome Second. Traduit par Hubert Elie avec la collaboration de Lothar Kelkel et René Schérer. Paris: Presses Universitaires de France, 1961.
Ihde, Don. *Hermeneutic Phenomenology.* Evanston: Northwestern University Press, 1971.
Kant, Immanuel. *Critique of Pure Reason.* Translated by Norman Kemp Smith. New York: St. Martin's Press, 1965.
—. *Religion Within the Limits of Reason Alone.* Translated by Theodore Breene and Hoyt Hudson. New York: Harper & Row, 1960.
Kockelmans, Joseph J. *Martin Heidegger, a First Introduction to His Philosophy.* Pittsburgh: Duquesne University Press, 1965.

—. *Phenomenology*. New York: Doubleday & Company, 1967.

Kwant, Remy. *Phenomenology of Language*. Pittsburgh: Duquesne University Press, 1965.

Lapointe, François H. "A Bibliography of Paul Ricœur," *Philosophy Today*, Vol. 16 (Spring, 1972), 28-33.

Merleau-Ponty, Maurice. *Phenomenology of Perception*. Translated by Colin Smith. New York: The Humanities Press, 1962.

—. *Signs*. Translated by Richard C. McCleary. Evanston: Northwestern University Press, 1964.

—. *Signes*. Paris: Gallimard, 1960.

Mohanty, J. N. *Edmund Husserl's Theory of Meaning*. Martinus Nijhoff: The Hague, 1964.

Nabert, Jean. *Éléments pour une éthique*. Paris: Presses Universitaires de France, 1943.

—. *Essai sur le mal*. Paris: Presses Universitaires de France, 1955.

Palmer, Richard. *Hermeneutics*. Evanston: Northwestern University Press, 1969.

Philibert, Michel. *Ricœur*. Paris: Editions Seghers, 1971.

Poncelet, Albert. A Review of *Finitude et culpabilité*. *International Philosophical Quarterly*, I (1961), 713-24.

Rasmussen, David M. *Mythic-Symbolic Language and Philosophical Anthropology*. The Hague: Martinus Nijhoff, 1971.

Richardson, William. *Heidegger, Through Phenomenology to Thought*. Martinus Nijhoff: The Hague, 1963.

Sallis, John C. *The Concept of the World: A Study in the Phenomenological Ontology of Martin Heidegger*. Thesis (Ph. D.) Tulane University of Louisiana.

—. *The Doctrine of the Ego in the Philosophies of Edmund Husserl and Jean-Paul Sartre*. New Orleans, 1962. Thesis (M.A.) Tulane University of Louisiana.

—. "Phenomenology and Language." *Personalist*. *XLVIII* (Autumn, 1967), 490-508.

Scanlon, John Daniel. *Husserl's Conception of Philosophy as a Rigorous Science*. New Orleans, 1968. Thesis (Ph. D.), Tulane University of Louisiana.

Schérer, René. *La phénoménologie des "recherches logiques" de Husserl*. Paris: Presses Universitaires de France, 1967.

Schillebeeckx, E. *God and the Future of Man*. Translated by N. D. Smith. Sheed and Ward: New York, 1968.

Sokolowski, Robert. *The Formation of Husserl's Concept of Constitution*. Martinus Nijhoff: The Hague, 1964.

Spiegelberg, Herbert. *The Phenomenological Movement*. Martinus Nijhoff: The Hague, 1965.

Stewart, David. "Paul Ricœur and the Phenomenological Movement." *Philosophy Today*, XII (Winter, 1968), 227-35.

Thévenaz, Pierre. *What Is Phenomenology? and Other Essays*. Translated by James M. Edie, Charles Courtney, and Paul Brockelman. Quadrangle Books: Chicago, 1962.

Vansina, Dirk. "Esquisse, orientation et signification de l'entreprise philosophi-
    que de Paul Ricœur," *Revue de Métaphysique et de Morale,* LXIC (March-
    July, 1964), 179-208 (July-October, 1964), 205-332.
Whitehead, Alfred North. *Symbolism, Its Meaning and Effect.* New York:
    Capricorn Books, 1959.

INDEX